LIVING IN A BODY ON A PLANET:
Your Divine Abilities

BY WILLIAM LINVILLE

I dedicate this book to my wholly divine, beautiful, benevolent bride, Mary, whom I love with all my heart. Thank you for all of your love and undying support, for walking side by side with me, and for your beautiful, priceless heart.

ACKNOWLEDGEMENTS

This book took two years to complete and was made possible by the assistance of many dear ones.

I dictated the first draft to Veronika Schulz-Barlow, who spent a year transcribing my initial dictation and making the changes I requested. The initial draft ran to over 350 pages.

I wanted this to be a book that would reach as many dear ones as possible, and I soon realized that I had material for more than one book. Michael Connell, Joseph Palermo and Deborah Bohn read the first draft of the manuscript and each made suggestions on what to include in this volume. They assisted me by reading and commenting on the initial draft.

Deborah Bohn took an additional year to edit the original 350 page manuscript down to its current length. She combined existing chapters with taped, videotaped and live interviews, and revised the text to produce a new manuscript. Joseph Palermo read and commented on the book each step of the way. Michael Connell completed the process of getting the book formatted and printed.

I wish to extend my thanks and love for all of their divine contributions.

TABLE OF CONTENTS

INTRODUCTION

My name is William Linville. I am what is known as a "walk in," one who enters the body of another as that person steps out of the physical. The body that I now have used to weigh over 425 pounds. It belonged to the person I refer to as "the old William Linville." My journey as a "walk in" began on a surgery table in California on December 20, 1996. The old William Linville was undergoing the surgical procedure known as gastric bypass. He very much did not want to experience the pain of recovering from surgery. During the operation, the old William left the body and I took his place.

As of six months prior to the surgery, the old William and I had begun having conversations about his journey in the physical and how he had gotten to the point of wanting to leave the body. He had many questions about why his life was the way that it was. He saw all of the opportunities that he had been given to awaken from his unhappiness, as well as all of the karmic agreements he had made that were still awaiting resolution. He saw that he could allow himself to break the chains of karma; he saw that he was in a dream he could wake up from. He was given clarity and the offer of assistance to go beyond what he had been taught. But because of all that he had experienced—from his time in the womb, through his childhood, and into adulthood—the old William decided that he would rather step out of this body, and return to the planet in the body of an Indigo child.

Once the old William had made his decision, he still had old paradigmal, i.e., karmic issues to resolve. We spent these six months of his sleep hours together in communion and communication. The agreement was made that he would step out of the physical and make a full transition. I would undergo stepping into his body, taking on the agreements and issues that he had, bringing them to resolution. In exchange for resolving the old William's karmic issues, I would step into a body for the first time.

I didn't know at first that I was the "new Will." I only knew that something very powerful had occurred and that I was very different. When I awoke in my hospital room, I recall the density I felt, the extreme heaviness. It was the oddest experience, as I was suddenly weighted down by the earth. I turned on the television and tried to watch a football game, as this was a great source of enjoyment for the old William. But I soon found it made no sense. Having no interest, I turned the TV off and looked to my left. There I saw my first sunset. I instantly felt so at peace, so at home in the omnipotence of creation! Then the old William's family came in. This was another odd experience. I recognized their roles: the mother, the wife, the brother, and all the others. Yet although I knew what parts they played, I really had no idea who they were.

The body was in a lot of pain, obviously, from the surgical procedure. And in the next few months the body turned upon itself, began to eat itself away, all the way through to the eyesight, the brain chemistry, the musculature, down to the cells. No one in the medical profession knew what to do, what was going on, or how to stop it. As the body went through this breakdown, everything at the same time was becoming more and more heightened for me, until I fully realized who I was. The body got to such a point that there was nothing to do but let go completely to either die off or be regenerated.

The days went by as my "new" (and first) body began to break down, organ by organ. Every system began to shut down. For two and a half years I remained in a wheelchair. There were many medical attempts to heal the body and take care of the symptoms, yet nothing seemed to work. The brain was broken down from all of the different forms of medication, while the many surgeries caused the body to shut down. At one point cardiac arrest took place. These illnesses were actually the dissolvement of old cellular memories that were not of love, light, or clarity, but that of anger, grief, confusion, and pain. During all of the pain, the symptoms and physical issues, the body was releasing the old William's memories and old karmic emotional states as well. After I was able to let those karmic issues be resolved, I was able to move into the body completely. Then I could be fully embodied.

Once I fully embodied, I began to have one-on-one conversations with all of the old William's family and friends. Those in his monad—a family made up of a karmic soul group—were very confused by what was happening to their son, husband, brother, friend. They knew the old William was no longer there. Their eyes could see the body of William, but the old William's presence was gone completely. As time passed, as I became more at home in the physical, the body's appearance changed completely. I lost more than 250 pounds, my eyesight returned, and I left my wheelchair. The physical mannerisms of the body vehicle changed completely as well. The family and friends of the old William saw that I was no longer part of their dynamic, but had truly become someone else.

In my talks with the old William's monad, I gave them clarity and guidance as to what had really happened to the old William. I offered them the clarity and assistance to move forward and to wake up. It was such a wake-up call for all concerned, offering them the grand opportunity to embody their wholeness and live in their fullest of potential as I was living in mine. And when we were complete, I left the life of the old William Linville behind to live as the new William Linville—the being that I am. Most everyone calls me Will.

For the next few years I assisted humanity in California. I attended massage school so that I could communicate with dear brothers about their physicality and assist them to live fully, to let the body be the body. During this time, I began to feel a presence. This presence would come to me at different times, especially in the evening and early morning hours when I was alone. This went on for almost three years, while I assisted dear ones. And then I came to Las Vegas to do my first speaking engagement. There in the front row was my angel, Mary. Here was that presence I had been sensing, right before me in the flesh. I like to say that when we met, I came home to her, because once I entered her home, I never left! We were married in May 2004. Today I live with my bride in Las Vegas, Nevada, assisting dear ones all over the world to awaken into this whole new life that is before them.

Some of you may wonder how I can address the issues of brother humanity when I haven't been through the usual birth to adulthood scenario. Please remember how much I have experienced since I came into this body. There have been moments of extreme physical pain. Then there were all of the surgeries this body endured, all the physical transformations. At one time the body was blind and wheelchair-bound, given only a few months to live. Now I walk five or ten miles a day. I don't live on some mountaintop, sheltered from other dear brothers and this world. I have lived in mansions and planted luscious gardens; at other times I slept on someone's floor. I experienced intense family dynamics with the old Williams's soul group. Now I am a loving husband who lives in a neighborhood, shops at the grocery store, changes the kitty litter and takes out the trash. The time I have spent in this physicality has been rich with experiences. In fact, if I hadn't experienced all of these things and so much more, seen how much there is to be celebrated and embraced and enjoyed in a body on a planet, I might not be speaking to you now.

Many ask, "Were you an entity that took over William Linville's body?" The best answer I can give is, "No." I'm not an entity, nor a soul. I am an essence that has come into this physical embodiment. Others ask, "Why are you here?" I am here to assist humanity to wake up and remember their complete divinity and omnipotence. I am here to assist in the divine marriage of the higher and lower selves. I am here to assist dear brothers with the knowledge that they can rebuild organs and cells, connect with their Creator essence, live their lives in the world but not of it. I am here to assist dear brothers to acknowledge that life is to be enjoyed and celebrated. The planet is forever changing to further accommodate your journey and expansion.

I am not superior because I'm a "walk in." I inhabit a body just as other dear ones do, and I don't hold myself apart. What a disservice that would be! Please remember we all have our own uniqued journeys, and no two are the same. We are all uniqued facets of divinity. We all have our roles to play, and I am merely here to assist. This book is written for your assistance, because it is easy for you to forget why you're here on this planet. It's easy to forget that you are the presence, the brilliance, the light Beingness. If only you could see the power you are, your realms of gold, your realms of light! If only you could know the power and the abilities each of you has within you as a being with a mind in a body on a planet.

When you become <u>You</u>, mind, body and spirit are united. When you live as this mind-body-spirit trinity, every facet of life opens up around you, and abundance comes in, relationships come in. This is what's taking place within you now, a brilliant new beginning. You feel the stirring as you let yourself be presented with everything that has been waiting to come to you from your natural states, your higher levels. Your divine essence is expanding exponentially. It is a state of fluidity that comes as you embody the presence of Creator that you are.

I am here to assist as critical mass has been reached. Critical mass is the point where humanity came together as a brotherhood, as a camaraderie, and decided to move forth in a whole different direction. This means that right now 81.3% of brother humanity is beginning a whole different journey, moving away from the sex-power-greed scenarios of the past. This silent agreement is completely and totally affecting the whole of brother humanity as more and more dear ones begin to step up, to step into their own journey, to walk their own walk. This has so much to do with the functionability of this world. Because as many more dear brothers begin to walk their walk and begin to run forward, it affects all of humanity.

This book is written as a guide to assist in your continual expansion, to remind you that you are eternal. Your eternal Beingness has always been available to you, and it is available to you now more than ever. You can let yourself fully and completely flourish with it, and begin to emanate exponentially. The state of neutrality, of becoming your own presence, is truly your natural state. I want to remind you that you have so many divine abilities—most of all the ability to live in that neutrality, in a beautiful clear state.

As you read, remember that the old world is gone, or more to the point, you have grown beyond it. Just by reading this book you have grown beyond it. The old rules no longer apply. Even in the calling to read this book you've moved beyond the past; looking forward you are embodying your divine essence and true essence itself. Whether you realize it consciously or unconsciously doesn't really matter. It's You calling yourself forward, calling forth the elements of divinity that you have been searching for and requesting. Some of you are more conscious of the calling than others, and you wonder why. But it doesn't really matter how you got here. What matters is that you are here now.

As everything continues to open and open and open for you, it is neutrality that's letting everything open. When you are shown, not from an outside source, not from an outside deity, but from the permission you've given yourself—you start to see so much further. Now two plus two is not necessarily going to equal four any longer. Or maybe we're throwing out two plus two. At one time that <u>did</u> serve, but you've outgrown it. Even by reading this book and starting to explore its meaning, you're outgrowing the old ways, the old thoughts. By the time you are at the end of this book, I can promise you will have outgrown the world as it has been, and you will be stepping into a new world as Creator, embodying yourself within creation.

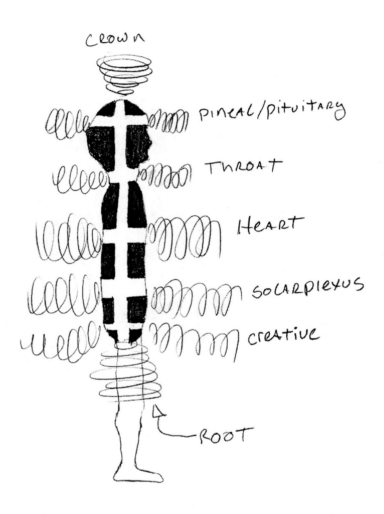

The three lower chakras are about the body; they represent the lower self. The three higher chakras represent the essence, the higher self. The higher and lower selves meet at the heart chakra, the heart center.

Chapter 1

WHERE DID WE COME FROM?

Before we begin to talk about your abilities, let's speak about where humanity has been and how humanity's journey is changing. You are all creatures of boundless magnificence, yet few of you recognize this. Some of you are just beginning to realize how magnificent you are, how powerful you are. The life stream you came in with had one perceptional outcome when it was based in a karmic resonance. Now into your life stream, your stream of consciousness, comes a stream of light, of divinity into your personal world. For the first time humanity <u>as a whole</u> has the power to ascend. Because the world has changed, and you have changed with it, you are in a state of total and complete expansiveness. Things in your life are beginning to shift, beginning to move, beginning to open. And every shift opens your life stream further.

For many thousands of years the presence of karma was so strong it was inescapable for all but a very few masters. Karma is the very definition of balances that have been out of balance. It is about trying to make up for, to reach a certain equilibrium, a zero point with another, and a zero point with yourself. Lifetimes would be spent playing different parts for one another in an effort to wake up. For example, in one lifetime you would play the thief, and in the next you would play the victim, and on and on, playing with different dear brothers through many life streams.

You would be born into a certain monad—a family made up of a karmic soul group. When you were ready to embark on a whole new journey through a physicality, you would be encouraged to be born into the monad that was the most rigid and confining, and the toughest for you. This could help ensure that you were not going to get caught up again in a reciprocal karmic cycle. Being born into that kind of monad could cause you to break free, to resolve your issues with that soul group and move beyond it into a whole new cycle. In this way the rigidity and confinement could be a source of expansion and growth. But the downside was that you might become trapped in one monad level, doing the same thing over and over and over with the same souls for many lifetimes.

Karma was engrained at such a deep level of consciousness because of the karmic grid system. This grid system was a magnetic structure that held everything in place to dominate, dictate, and define you in each life stream. It really defined where you were on your own journey and where you would go, how you would act and react. The karmic grid system ran your thought forms so that you might move just a bit further along in each life stream, settling some karmic debts and acquiring others.

We will spend much of this book looking at the union of your higher and the lower levels. The higher levels, located in the three highest chakras, are about total and complete expansiveness, all-inclusive, without separation. The higher levels are about camaraderie, compassion and enjoyment. Karma is based in the three lower chakras where the "me, me, me" levels of consciousness reside. The lower levels are what created the karmic grid system. When separation began, the lower levels, the little me, the false me, took command. That's when the ego was created. This is where the perception began that the mind is real. Another false perception—that you are your mind—also began at this time. These levels are all about separation, about one's own personal journey. The little me is preoccupied with sex, power, and greed. These levels are all about satisfying egoic desires.

Now remember that the "me, me, me" level of consciousness started out to be about survival. This little me is the part that says, "I think, I should, I ought, I must, I have to, I've got to, I need to." If you notice, it's one linear state of consciousness based in the physical. This is because the mind was created to assist you to be able to take care of the physicality in the most benevolent way, which helped you enjoy the physicality to its fullest of potential. The mind was created to be able to use its abilities for protection, so the body would not step off cliffs, or allow itself to be consumed by the dinosaur realm, or succumb to the effects of weather and the elements. The mind <u>does</u> complement. It is the ego states and beliefs that do not.

So how does the ego work? It is created with emotion and judgment. The ego is created in the third trimester in the womb; as you enter the body principle, you make decisions about yourself based on what was going on in the womb. Although ego has no power unless given power, it has a way of making you believe everything it tells you. One ego may say, "I'll never be enough. I'll never have enough." Another ego says, "I'm better than you. I deserve more than you." And these egos are drawn together. Some believe that someone with a "big" ego thinks he's better than everyone. But the funny part is, the person who thinks he isn't good enough has a big ego too. Both of them are ruled by their egos, and the only difference is in what their egos say.

Now this separation, this takeover by the ego, was caused by being "stuck" in the grid: identification with the physicality, identification with gender principles, identification with the idea that more is better. As these sex-power-greed scenarios were born, the lower levels took control: "I want what you have—I should have what you have! So I'll take your belongings and make them mine, take your bride or your husband. I'm even going to attempt to enslave you, or end your life stream."

So how might that play out? Let's say that 14 lifetimes ago you were walking in the green fields. And we see you moving through the meadow with your bow and arrows bringing forth dinner for that evening. And suddenly, for no apparent reason another dear brother appears, takes all of your belongings and assists you off the planet. Now where did that come from? Was it by chance? Was it by primal nature? Was it about survival?

You have been told that this was about a "survival of the fittest." Actually, it wasn't about survival. It was all about a karmic agreement. There was plenty of food to go around for all concerned and more, where everyone could be sitting at the table feasting on one delicacy after another. But here we had a karmic journey about past life scenarios. And let's take it further. Why would this dear brother have ever acted out this behavior? Why did you have a feeling of familiarity with this dear brother? Why would you be feeling this from your body's solar plexus down, from the diaphragm state down? Because your relationship with this dear brother was based within the adrenals and survival, within your cellular structures as well as your soul level. Your meeting began to activate your body and certain remembrances because you knew that this was about a karmic agreement being brought to resolution.

What about the possibility of another outcome? What would have happened if he had made a different decision? Let's say that the dear brother came out of the forest and decided that he really did not need your belongings. What if he decided that he would not go against himself any longer? It would have been a done deal. The whole soul, karmic agreement, contract, would have dissolved, and it would have been a completely different outcome for you and the dear one you were assisting to come to resolution. Even though everything seemed preordained, that dear brother was being offered the opportunity to step beyond the grid system.

Even in that glimpse of thought, if the dear brother had the clarity to see himself in truth as Creator Incarnate, he would have resolved the karma and stepped outside the grid. What kept these battles, these conflicts, continually acting out was intense emotion from the soul level, the cellular level, the molecular level. But everyone had that glimpse of an opportunity to go beyond it. Their higher levels were always attempting to step in, offering different ways and opportunities to dissolve these agreements before they were acted out. Nevertheless, because you had now disengaged, you took yourself three realms higher when you were stepping through the astral planes of consciousness after leaving the physicality. Another journey and agreement, i.e., contract, achieved and completed.

To explain the power of the karmic grid system, let me speak for a moment about cellular memories. Cellular memories are like experiences stored within the cells, ties to certain activities and scenarios you've been through. These memories are more heightened than others, more emotional perhaps for whatever reason; they have been locked into the cells, some for survival, some for bliss. The first time that I experienced fish was with my bride, at our first dinner together. She served salmon and mushrooms with olive oil and beautiful greeneries. I say that "I" had never tried fish, but my body had. You see, the old William Linville fully and completely despised fish, and that cellular memory was present for me as well. At one time in childhood he had been forced to eat something he didn't wish to eat. All that emotion, the feeling of confinement, of having no control, was forced into the experience of eating fish.

As our meal progressed to the first bite of salmon, you could have heard the ringing throughout the Universe!

It was the most priceless, elegant feast that I have ever had on this planet. When I let go of the emotion, just allowing my body to taste the delicious fish, those cellular memories dissolved. Exploring with clarity, I felt the dissolvement of that density within my cellular structure and cellular memories. Just as the physicality can dissolve its cellular memories, you can dissolve ties to the karmic grid system in this incarnation.

Now let's honor the karmic grid system and how it was created because it has had an effect on you and everyone else. And the purpose of karma, the reason behind karma, was to get your own attention, to allow you to wake up. But the magnetic separation that caused the ego to be created also created the "I think, I should, I ought, I must" thought patterns that rule most dear brothers to this day. So you just stepped out of the physical time after time, learning from some experiences, sometimes moving forward, but so often staying locked in those magnetics.

We have seen that karma was shaped by the sex-power-greed scenarios and by out-of-control emotional states. And that's where judgment came in. Judgment began to separate you further and further from your true self, to polarize you. It kept you from your Universalis states, the marriage of higher and lower. And throughout your life streams judgment would begin to slow down the functionability of the organs, of the brain, of processability, of your own clarity. The body would begin to shut itself down, one judgment after another. For one judgment always leads to another, just constant judgment on all levels, constantly polarizing you, turning you against yourself and others:

"I'm not a good mother."

"I'm not a good husband."

"I don't have enough. What is wrong with me?"

"Why does she have more than me?"

"I deserve more. I should be richer."

"I wish I were beautiful."

"He's no good."

"She shouldn't act that way."

"I hate my job. I can never do what I want."

When a judgment is made, a deity is created. This deity, the judgment solidified, is something that you deem to make a reality. It is the true meaning behind the self-fulfilling prophecy. A dear brother will tell me, "I hope my car doesn't break down in this heat!" He becomes a little obsessed about it. Every time we speak, he mentions his fears about the car vehicle. Sure enough, it ends up in the repair shop, and the dear brother sees this as a symptom of his awful luck. I have to chuckle at this one, because as Creator Incarnate, that dear brother is making his own reality. You make these deities into a part of your life without ever being aware, and you constantly give them power. And as you give your power away, it affects every part of you. Deities create more complex structures. Suddenly there is a mass consciousness, and you must fit in with the mass consciousness beliefs—not to thrive, but to survive. And the mass consciousness affects everyone. This "reality" continues to play and play, present and present. You react to it emotionally, physically, in every way. But the term "reality" is not quite accurate. The only part that ever gives it life is you as Creator commanding it so.

Now, bringing forward my beloved friend Mr. Yeshua ben Joseph (Jesus), he was very clear when he came in. The power of his story is not that he was the Chosen One, but he listened to that Voice. He listened to that knowing. He did not give his power away to perceptional phantoms called emotion and judgment. He didn't deny emotion, he denied its power. His mastery was in walking his walk each day. Consider this: Emotion, judgment, and ego are alive in your body vehicle right now. But they have no power at all, unless you give them power.

This incarnation is the sum of all the brilliant life streams that you've walked through, your past lives, playing different parts for brother humanity, wearing many different hats. You've played the victim and the victimizer over and over again; you may have played these roles through hundreds and hundreds of lifetimes. This comes to you when you're experiencing déjà vu, when you have a certain familiarity with something you've never experienced before. You can feel the past experience. How many dear brothers have irrational fears and are afraid of things yet they don't know why? It can be fear of a certain animal, or fear of going in the water, or a sudden sense of dread. You may love someone instantly, or instantly dislike the dear brother, seemingly out of nowhere. These past life streams have been running so much of this life stream. But their hold on you is now being dissolved.

We've spoken of cellular memories and emotional states. We've spoken about incarnational journeys. Emotion has a consciousness. It is a life force. It was that giant boogeyman who was hiding in your closet.

But he has been exposed; he's no longer in charge. Now you're presented with your own guidance and clarity about emotion to go beyond emotion, to let yourself rise above it. What are these brilliant memories that have been surfacing for you? Where have these memories been coming from in the first place? These are dimensions that you were still experiencing within. This is the part that has kept you magnetically and karmically in a state of repetition until you began to wake up. That's where these memories are coming from. They are being cleansed on every level. This is why your guidance realms can now let their presence be known. You are becoming lighter than the density, beginning to embody and embrace the omnipotence of All That Is. "Thank you, but no thank you," you say when the emotions come up. "I give you no power."

You used to have roots that were magnetically, karmically integrated inside this magnetic planetary grid system. There are no longer those roots, because you are coming home. Harmonic convergence occurred in 1987. This is when the karmic grid was dissolved. And since this convergence the whole globe, all the continents, the diversities of brother humanity have been coming together to fully complement one another. This represents the dissolvement of segregation, the dissolvement of separation, a coming together of all humanity from a harmonious state. Notice how so much in the media in these last few years has been about global events? Our response says we will not accept anything less than camaraderie, peace and harmoniousness. There have been so many challenges, and so many challenges to come. But dear brothers are coming together every day to assist each other, and to share their hearts with one another. Think of the tsunamis, the earthquakes, the hurricanes that have come and gone in the past few years. How has humanity responded? They've responded with an outpouring of love, compassion, money, clothes, and sustenance.

And remember that this harmonic convergence was voted unanimously by every dear one on the planet. Now it's free time, it's time for you to get to play and to express and remember and embody You. The freedom for You to embody the complete marriage of the higher and the lower. This is you as Creator Incarnate, the Christ consciousness. It matters not what you call it, the important part is that this is you embodying your true essence. You are letting yourself become completely free and immune from the old world, so that you can wake up in this new world.

But please don't believe me. Don't take my word for it. Instead play with your consciousness. Examine the ideas here. As you're playing, you will see and remember. As you're playing you'll be feeling all these changes bubbling up. For some it's every particle of anger leaving, coming up to be exposed and dissolved. For some it's letting the sadness melt away. Whatever happens, it's a celebration of you stepping into You.

This change in the world is not about work, but about the absence of work. Everyone will experience it eventually. It may take many lifetimes, but everyone will experience the marriage of higher and lower. The question is, how many lifetimes would you like to take? Would you just like to experience this now? It has a lot to do with what you are willing to accept. You can step out of the world and let everything simply pass by, observe the world and have a blast. Or you can step right in, saying "Thank you, but no thank you," to the mind, dissolving emotional conflicts by bypassing the mind—and have a blast. You're here to play and celebrate your own divinity. So say, "Thank you" to the mind and the egoic structures. "Please feel free to come along all the way—from a higher state of consciousness."

So now you are living in a world without karma. What does that mean exactly? First of all, you're not limited to a time dynamic of learning and repetition. You waited eons to get here to be able to express, to be able to step out of the dogmatic responses and the ritualistic ceremonial approaches. As you are waking up, you can go beyond identification with an egoic structure. The ego-based world looks at everything as positive or negative, good or bad. That need not have power over you any longer. The polarized states you felt were identified with the karmic grid system and very much a part of it. Now your view of the outside world that has been based in survival can be brought to completion and resolution. And when you are not preoccupied with settling old scores, or learning lessons, that's when the real learning can take place.

This brings up an important point: You notice that most dear ones still seem to be struggling with that so-called non-existent karma. Perhaps you are struggling with karmic ties of your own. Remember sharing a holiday dinner with your family? There's proof that the feeling of karma still exists! But what if it doesn't have to be that way? What if it is the egoic mind, the lower levels that keep the memory of karma alive?

Imagine that you have a terrible relationship with your mother. She doesn't respect your wishes and always treats you like a child. You would like to create some distance, but you feel karmically bound to her. What would happen if you gave yourself the freedom to walk away when your mother treats you disrespectfully? What if you were no longer bound to her by a karmic obligation? As Creator Incarnate, you are making up the world each day. Without the burden of karma, you are free to find new ways to deal with your mother issues. No matter what your choice is, your freedom is the key.

You've been attempting to remember who you are and that there is so much more. And this is where you as Creator will be in the world but not of it. You are no longer of the world because you're not getting caught up in all of these little dynamics around you. Instead you'll have the freedom to see beyond the drama from an overview as Creator Incarnate. Your natural birthright is your right to enjoy prosperity, clarity, wide openness, communion, connectedness, full complete embodiment within the whole Universe. You were made to be one with All That Is, to enjoy prosperity from every direction, opening up your heart to the blissfulness and joy that has always been yours. There is truly nothing to work for, it is yours already. I call this giving yourself the go-ahead.

When you start to give yourself the go-ahead, you're giving yourself permission to receive this birthright. This is what you came here to explore. Going beyond the karmic deities, going beyond the, "I think, I should, I ought, I must, and I owe," moving into a

13

state of complete receiving and a giving in one. What would you like to receive? What would you like to give? It is natural to give from the heart. It is also natural to receive from experience your innate abilities. It is <u>not</u> your natural birthright to get pulled onto all of these emotional roller coasters. It <u>is</u> your natural birthright to enjoy all of creation and to have all of creation open up for you. When you give yourself this go-ahead, success is guaranteed.

All dear brothers from the equality state are offered every opportunity in this Universe to flourish, to succeed, to receive all the brilliant gifts and achieve all the dreams they could have ever imagined and beyond. It is a world without wanting, the complete world of having and enjoying, putting oneself forth to fully, completely receive all the gifts the Universe has to offer. It's just that you must be willing to let it happen without getting mentally and emotionally engaged. But that's where the "F" word comes in: Free will. Are you giving the go-ahead? There are two different pathways here that you are free to take. The first path involves you stepping into You. The second path is about attempting to stay where you've been playing. I have to chuckle at that one, because you've gone beyond the old playground. But that's okay. Play wherever you choose to play, but please do know that you've already outgrown the past, and you're going to propel forward no matter what you do.

As you move into a new level of consciousness, you let the Universe begin to present for you from your guidance realms, your angelic and archangelic presences. You are moving into a state without the little me, where there's openness to All That Is. And this is where your true life, your eternal nature, and the whole world begins to open for you. The body becomes your friend, the mind becomes your friend, and you are in touch with your Creator consciousness. At the final level of complete embodiment, you can be in total and complete enjoyment 24 hours a day.

Chapter 2

WHERE ARE WE GOING?

Before we speak more about your divine abilities, it may assist to speak about God. Almost every dear one on the planet has some concept of God and the divine. So who—or what—is God? The God of the mass consciousness was created as a deity from a polarized state. Take the God of Christianity, who works more as a father figure; this mind-created outside deity serves as justifier and judge, there to condemn or approve of you. This deity is there to decide whether you are worthy or unworthy of the ascension process, whether you are worthy or unworthy to be greeted at the metaphoric pearly gates. This is the same God that was created to control your behavioral mannerisms. It was created to condemn you if you misbehaved, and to honor you if you were good. And being "good" can be defined as being a follower. This God was a man-made deity created for control. The same is true of all religions, of gods and goddesses. This type of "god" is about the absence of love.

The God that we are referring to within this book is the facet of Creator essence that You are. This God, call it the central sun, call it the diamond in the sky, call it the ruler—this deity is a presence that you feel. We refer to it so often throughout this book, as the presence of oneness, of communion, of wholeness, the embodiment of Creator Incarnate. Your Creator essence is based in a total and complete unconditional love state. You can do no wrong. You can do no right. Instead you can play as the deity, the facet, the brilliance that You are. <u>This</u> is your natural birthright, rather than the man-made God that taught you to behave or be condemned.

The God we have been speaking of—call it your higher levels, call it your presence, call it your absence—has given you the right to be in your fullest of potential, the right to play with your innate abilities, the right to receive all the gifts this whole Universe has to offer. It is your right to offer the exquisite divinity of self-expression. This God gives you the right to succeed and flourish, the right to recognize the knowingness of All That Is. You realize it is also your right to love and to be loved, to enjoy and be enjoyed, to receive and to give. What is most important: You have the right of complete and total self-acceptance, no matter what may be happening in your out-picturing world.

You have the right to hear your own voice and learn what <u>You</u> want, rather than accepting as necessary all of these metaphoric levels of achievement. These are the things you were taught must be achieved before you could begin to be happy. But now you no longer have to lie. And your true "responsibility" is to love and to enjoy. The natural innate abilities you are recognizing are the God-given rights that have been yours since you first decided to come in to the physical. These are the God-given rights that have come with You, from You, and to You as Creator Incarnate waking up through creation. Living with these rights is truly your natural state.

The funny part is, living with and recognizing your God-given rights may feel really unnatural, especially at first. You have the right—everyone has the right—to choose an individual path. And even though the mass consciousness discourages it, I ask you this question: How many Picassos, Einsteins, or Edisons does it take to see that taking a new path is a wonderful thing? Now those dear brothers all turned out to be quite success-ful in mass consciousness terms. But what if the situa-tion is different? What if someone doesn't care about the standard type of "success"? The mass conscious-ness belief says that certain paths are wrong. Although these beliefs are slowly expanding as more and more brothers wake up, many dear ones still believe that they must please others or follow a certain formula to be happy. So they keep trying to fit in where they don't really belong. They don't recognize that they have rites of passage to play in so many diverse realms of creation.

When you open yourself to explore and question further, you'll start to find your own facet, your own remembrance of God and what God means to you. There is no pass or fail, good or bad, right or wrong answer. It is the God who is waking up within You, as You, through You. This God is your friend, your com-rade, your caretaker, your care <u>holder</u>. This is the God who supports you no matter what is going on in your life stream, the one who will compassionately pick you up off your knees, assist you to go beyond stumbling, who is always in a state of forgiveness, communion, and camaraderie. As you begin to step into your heart level, as you begin to step into your own presence, your own innate abilities, you will find the God that you have been seeking. So let's look at some of these God-given, innate abilities. Please remember that you have so many other abilities as well! You have been perfection ever since you were born into a body on this planet; you are truly unlimited.

- You have the ability to enjoy wonderful relationships. This ability starts with learning how and why to live beyond the emotions. You can have unhealthy relationships with food, with substances, with other people, and with yourself. Your emotions have been based in the way the outside world judges experiences. Those judgments from the outside world truly have nothing to do with you and what your life can look like.

- You have the ability to rebuild your DNA and raise your vibratory structures. By accessing levels of brain chemistries, you can assist the body to rebuild itself. This will bring it to optimum health and well-being and homeostasis through the constant reproduction of health, youth and vitality.

- You have the ability to play with much higher states of consciousness. This ability is about going beyond the mind, opening up to new worlds, and opening up to your natural innate abilities. This is what people such as Einstein, Benjamin Franklin and Picasso have done.

- You have the ability to re-create a communion with your angelic realms, your archangelic realms, and the ascended host realms. These dear ones are right there before you and have been waiting to let their presence be known to you. They want to provide their assistance to you, to be instrumental in your life stream. You have the ability to recognize them and be open to their guidance.

- You have the ability to communicate with all of the kingdoms. Because everything is living consciousness, you can communicate with the plant kingdom, the oceanic kingdom, the animal kingdom, the minerals, the soils, and every other kingdom on the planet, while letting them communicate back to you.

All of humanity have these abilities if they would just listen to their nudges and follow them. While you do not need to meditate to do this, meditation was created as a way to bypass the mind and to let the body regenerate. Isn't that a very beautiful gift? It was a gift to let the nudges become louder so you could notice and follow them. Rather than moving away to a place of peace in the mountains of Tibet, you can now follow your nudge and have peace everywhere. Now you can let Tibet take place right here, enjoy everything and have a blast along the way with all of your beautiful friends, with all of humanity around you. You can be open to everything that presents, from all of creation, because you're welcoming in love from every area of your life. You don't have to be alone or in charge anymore. Remember, you have so many dear ones and so much available for you, as You. Simply welcome everything in.

The experiential realms exist for your entertainment, enjoyment, expressiveness and embodiment. These realms also exist to allow your body vehicle to fully and completely explore. Of course, not every experience is positive. In every full life there is bound to be unhappiness, annoyance and anger. The mind level is still there. But an experiential realm is just an experience. There's no judgment in place. It is a journey, an unfoldment. An experience is openness, and at times it is even a wake-up call. But as you just simply let it be, in that state of simplicity it is completely and totally available to be enjoyed.

Imagine you are out driving on one of those days when all the dear brothers seem to be speeding, and cutting you off, and you can feel the road rage building. You are feeling all of these physical sensations in your body. Now you can react with rage against the next person who cuts you off, or you can not react. You can simply say, "Namaste, dear brother," and continue to enjoy your drive. And you will find that the rage drains out of you, just like that. Because why would you want to ruin even a moment of your day by letting your lower levels take over? What a disservice that would be to yourself and everyone around you. And once you let go of the judgment that you should get angry, the physicality returns to normal.

It's a beautiful beginning point, a beautiful complement, even starting to say and see that you have different abilities to change how you feel. But what you're doing beyond that is allowing your true essence to come to the forefront. This creates changes throughout your lifestream. You actually become your own guru. (Gee, you are You!) You're playing with your innate abilities, continuing to become comfortable living beyond the mind level. You're also bringing the mind level along, because as the mind starts to realize that you have these abilities, it lets you be more of the director. The mind then allows you to see what takes place, rather than insisting on some controlled state of how it should be, how it has to be, how it needs to be. With judgment removed, you are free to express.

You all have your own ways of looking at and being in the world. I call this your uniquedness. Your expressed uniquedness is in your desires, your clarities, your enjoyments. It's the way that you present yourself in a body on a planet—your body structure, the way you speak, your coloring. It's in the resonating vibratory levels of the body structure, the emanation that you're offering to this world as the facet of Creator that you are. But it goes so far beyond your physicality. For each and every facet of Creator has such brilliant diversities. Each brings forth a certain tone, a certain vibratory level, from colors to consciousness, to particles of light—each human being has its own unique signature.

To appreciate each dear one for his or her uniquedness, you merely must be willing to look at judgment and emotion for what they are. When you ask, "Show me the truth," now you are freeing yourself from all the disillusionment, moving into complete clarity with everything. You are not creating another belief or a perceptional judgment about what is being presented. You are in a total neutrality state. Because what we're doing is simply flying, letting changes take place around us, doors shutting over here, other ones opening up over there, saying goodbye to some dear ones, saying hello to some others. This is possible because at the same time you are not becoming engaged and hooked in to these different realms.

You may have been feeling separation, in many different ways, in your outside world realm. Because, remember, you're also at the forefront of living this new kind of existence that is affecting all of these other dear brothers in your life stream, offering the opportunity for them to step up as well. Some people are going to be experiencing energetic vortex levels of consciousness, opening, opening, opening just by being in your presence. You're going to be feeling yourselves vibrating faster than ever before. Hey bring it on, let's go! This can actually make you feel more separation for a while. But it really comes back to the permission that you are giving yourself to experience and begin to embody. The discomfort comes from your lack of familiarity. As you are letting yourself start to play with your innate abilities, I can promise you one hundred and fifty-thousand percent it's going to change!

So let's begin by breaking energy with everyone and everything as well as with the whole world. To break energy is to withdraw yourself from the mind, from the different scenarios and situations around you, and to let yourself begin to feel your own presence from a total clarity state, an open state of love. You can do this at any time to reconnect with your higher levels.

Begin by sliding your hands across each other in front of your heart, then pushing your right hand out while bringing your left palm to rest against your heart level. Focus on your heart chakra. You are breaking energy with the whole world as you've known it, also breaking energy with all the genetic monad scenarios, with planetary magnetics. You're breaking energy with all perceptional attachment to outcomes. This is bringing your consciousness right back through your body vehicle.

Now bring your attention to a part of your body. Whether your attention is on a hand, on the neck, even on a toe, it matters not. Bringing attention to that body part allows you to feel your own presence and welcome it to come forward again. Now you're disengaged from the mind and identities, stepping out of the world and out of time. You're also beginning to express and embody your natural state of neutrality, i.e., your eternal Beingness, the presence of Creator that you are.

For all those that are saying, "Well, I don't really feel anything. Are you making it up?" No, not at all. You're starting to open up passages, passageways, opportunities and acknowledgments. I call this the celebration of You. And the more you do this, the more you'll begin to feel. I know there are also those of you who ask, "Well how can I be celebrated? What could I have done or said to be celebrated?" And I say, it's your natural birthright. Just because you're in a body on a planet the celebration has already begun. What we're doing is welcoming forward the celebratory party to greet yourself. I know that many of you can feel something special happening—a clarity and a knowledge that keeps growing.

This is what happens when you're not working, you're not attempting to earn ascension or attempting to be worthy or having to work for these ascended hosts to be in your presence. You have been taught that you must jump through all of these hoops, to be a certain way. For some, communicating with ascended hosts was thought to be nonsense. And those who aspired to communicate were told they had to walk on a tight-wire of taught behavioral mannerisms. The funny part is that you had these dear ones around you, ready to give you assistance, clarity, and to walk side by side with you all along.

So here You come, looking through those eyes again from what I'd call your higher levels, your dimensional planes. The idea that you have these higher levels, it may seem a little bit egoic. Well, maybe it is, and maybe it isn't. But if the idea of higher levels is egoic, why are you getting to have the overview of everything, the big picture that allows you to see everything for what it is? Maybe this overview is there to show you who You really are. The perception has been that only certain people are special, and so only the seers, the sages, the masters, the priests and priestesses could connect with their higher levels. So once again please ask yourself, "Why would that be? Why would our Creator give such a separation to the holy, unholy, to the pure, and to the sinners? How could that ever be?"

If you believe in the Creator as communion, as oneness, as equality, how could all this power be given to some and not all? Because you were taught that you didn't have these abilities, you sit at the feet of others as they teach about their abilities. What would happen if you no longer sat at the feet of another? The world that is your birthright, that you were born into, is now available to you. You're letting that world come to you as you step into your abilities as Creator Incarnate.

I know some of you will want to stop right here because of your perceptional understandings of blasphemy. You may be asking yourself, "How can this ever be? How can I think of myself as Creator Incarnate?" And that's okay. But what are you feeling in your body as you read these words? What's going on in the room? What's going on in your outside world? Some of you might want to re-contemplate your response. Well, perhaps then this also means that you really <u>can</u> feel the way that you feel, and really <u>can</u> step into your own divinity. Call this your God-given rights, abilities, your birthright, it doesn't matter what you call this feeling, it's still you. I promise you—and mark every word—the calling will not go away.

When my good friend Yeshua (Jesus) talked about perseverance, it was not about becoming closed down to all the obstacles. It was about going beyond them, no matter what was going on in your outside world. It wasn't about stepping out of obstacles and conflicts, it was disengagement from obstacles, letting all the obstacles change to fully and completely complement. The idea is not, "I've got to keep trying, trying, trying, trying, trying, and maybe one day I'll get a break." That is not You. Once again, that type of thinking was taught. It's more about looking at the obstacle in a different way.

Your whole world is changing so much more than the mind could have ever comprehended. It's going to change much more than you could ever fathom, because you're letting your higher levels, your manifest levels, call it Creator, call it God, begin to give to you. You're beginning to receive their presence, companionship, and support. You're letting everything continue to open for you because you're giving yourself permission to play with and remember You.

Now I want to honor that many are going to read this and say, "Wow it's a little bit beyond me." That's the little mind talking. Absolutely, it's beyond your awareness at the mind level. But it's also being seen by the eternal You that has always been and will always be. Once again my challenge to you is to explore what is beyond the mind. As you're starting to re-integrate, watch what happens physically, mentally, and in every way. That old mental grasp is no longer being held in place, holding you back. That old mental grasp is no longer a necessity.

So you say to yourself, "Now I can begin to feel harmoniousness in my physicality and what's in my outside world, but could I still feel the harmoniousness in the middle of a battlefield? Can I feel the harmoniousness and be totally wide open to everything no matter where I'm at?" Well, a battlefield can be a very uncomfortable place. But the answer is, "Yes!" You could be on the battlefield, you could be in a giant corporate environment in the heart of Manhattan, you could be in the fields picking flowers or corn. The place or event doesn't really matter. You can still break energy, still feel open. You can feel your own essence, your own energy, without the necessity of putting up walls to protect the little self. And what happens when you're neither affected nor unaffected by the world? Could that mean you're completely open to the world?

Now I don't want to pretend that one situation might not feel different than another. Absolutely. There's a big difference between fighting on a battlefield and gazing at a sunrise. That's part of the beauty of life in a body on a planet. You are here to have experiences, and they may seem good and bad, pleasant and unpleasant. But that is your mind level. From your higher levels, why would anything less than brilliance come into your life stream? So how about you get out the champagne bottles, the chocolate cake, and celebrate? Celebrate the ending of the old ways of thinking, the ending of the karmic grid system, the ending of the personal conflicted states. Welcome in your higher levels, the beginning of the real You, the true You.

Why not be in the forefront of it? Take back your own power, your own divinity, and let yourself continue to move forward. Then watch what happens. Because I can promise you, your whole world will be real, not the version of the world that was taught and repeated. Not the one that was set up by brother humanity, your mother, your father, relatives, doctors, science, etc. You are becoming the presence, and as Creator Incarnate you are letting yourself begin to emanate exponentially through this world and beyond. Now you're truly becoming open to All That Is to be celebrated and enjoyed.

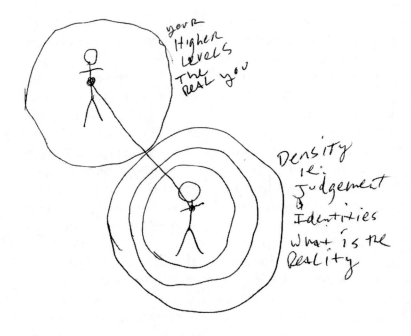

your
Higher
Levels
The
Real you

Density
i.e.
Judgement
&
Identities
What is the
Reality

Freedom from judgment is about recognizing the real You. The heart is connected to your higher levels. As you grow more in touch with these higher levels, you lose the density that comes from listening to the mind levels and the ego.

Chapter 3

WHAT IS A TRUE RELATIONSHIP, AND HOW CAN YOU HAVE ONE?

Before we begin to examine your ability to enjoy the most wonderful, loving relationships, it might assist to talk about what creates those not-so-wonderful ones. You have so many relationships—with others, with so-called inanimate objects, and with yourself. When a relationship is not so wonderful, it has everything to do with the mind, with the way the mind level functions when it thinks it's in charge. "I've got to do this, that, and the other," says the mind. And it thinks about responsibilities, rights and wrongs, and all the perceptional judgments it is making. The mind believes itself to be quite important!

We've already talked about the dissolving of the karmic grid, and the dissolving of karma along with it. So if karma is dissolved, then why do so many dear brothers still seem to be locked in karmic struggles? It's because for so many, the mind level is still in control. The mind level, with its beliefs, its perceptions, its judgments, is running their life streams. This may be true for you as well, but it doesn't have to be. The ability to enjoy brilliant, beautiful relationships is about getting the mind out of the way. It's about losing the beliefs, perceptions and judgments that have created so many outside deities, and learning to live in freedom.

First and foremost, you're at that point along your life stream when you're starting to wonder why you've been going to work, watching TV, doing the shopping, having a day off and doing the yard, etc. You find yourself being involved in one repetitive perceptional state after another without even realizing it. How are you supposed to be feeling that you're really not feeling? And haven't you also begun to question your own Beingness? You've made agreements, you've got to keep your word, you've got to be of the highest integrity, and you've got to continue to do all of this stuff that doesn't quite resonate with you anymore. As you start to re-contemplate yourself and your beliefs and repetitive behaviors as well, you begin to ask yourself, "Why am I doing these things, anyway?" This is not so much about being present, not so much about being clear, not so much about any of that. You are starting to question what is, because now what you're doing is moving toward a neutrality state.

The neutrality state has everything to do with wonderful relationships. It is about getting off that metaphoric daily grind, a grind that's actually not so metaphoric when you look around you. You see one dear brother after another going through the dating game, the mating game, putting on a front, putting on an act as they attempt to survive. What you're doing in the neutrality state is stepping back from the mass consciousness for a moment. You ask yourself why you are continually going through these scenarios that really don't resonate with you. You are starting to re-question: "Now why do I do what I'm doing when I'm doing it?"

Here's an example: If you go along with the way others tend to believe on this planet, you're supposed to buy into and accept everything your parents have to share, give, and teach. Then if your life doesn't work, you're going to blame them, create all this judgment and give them responsibility for your life not working out. You're still missing the point of the whole karmic message. So what if you started to re-contemplate? You might find that blaming your parents and your family for everything just doesn't seem quite accurate. It doesn't seem quite fair. And as you re-contemplate, it doesn't really seem that as the brilliant Creator you are, you would have chosen this path.

Why would you choose to be born into the family monad, the soul that you have chosen, even though you had the choice of three different families? What if your Creator was, and is, assisting you to arise and wake up from these family monads, to fully and completely let yourself be embraced beyond the monad and into your true divinity? What if all of what's dissolving is what is no longer true? What if the true Creator is now re-awakening itself through You, and as You, moving beyond the family monad and the old paradigmal grid system to fully open into a whole new paradigm?

Whatever would happen if you started to become different? What would happen if you were to step into your own? What if you were to re-contemplate that maybe you don't have to fit in anywhere? What if you began to question the whole aging process, question the nutritional elements, and began to question what has to be, and <u>why</u> it has to be? What if you were to question the whole physical makeup, molecular makeup, genetic makeup, and began to question how it works? Wouldn't that be a whole new exploration of all sorts of divine clarity? That would start a whole new life full of true meanings and benevolent experiences, and all sorts of new doors of abundance and love opening for you.

In the old karmic paradigm, before this opportunity was presented, your life would be just like this: You would step out of the womb scenario. You would go through the formative years, from infancy to toddlerhood, and on through the teenage years until you became an adult. With each year you would further create an in-depth state, what you'd call your own person, with your own individuality and identity. But the mass consciousness beliefs would also sink deeper into your mind. As you think of growing up, can you remember when things began feeling much denser? That "growing up" process turned what was once complete purity, divinity, particles of light, particles of gold, in and through a body principle, into the density of the mind, the world, the expectations of achievements that created a false self.

You would put on one mask after the other. Not just masks, but whole different life-forms of identifications, some that you were choosing, some taught, some on purpose, and some by default. You were taught to take on all of these personalities and identities. What would happen if you were no longer confined to that? What would happen if you started questioning who you are, and who made the masks real? Whoever defined "growing up"? Who said that you could not be wise until you're 58 years old? Whoever told you that you would only be grown into your physicality once you had reached a certain linear age? Whoever said that you had to indoctrinate your mind with all this data and information, all the beliefs "required" to function in a body on a planet?

I've known dear ones who spend the better part of their lives following the new age movement, going through all of these colorful processes to remove blockages and old programming. And it takes until the very end of their life streams before they feel free from all of the guilt and remorse that was taught. What would have happened if they became free without those colorful processes? What if they didn't have to wait? So what would happen if you started to be complete right now? And the biggest question of all: What would happen if you simply let go of belief?

A belief is a state of commanding a certain reality until it becomes truth. And as this "reality" becomes a truth it begins to affect your outside world, begins to affect how you feel about yourself. The funny thing is, a belief is a particle of consciousness, a live deity that <u>you</u> have given life. It cannot exist unless you command it so, and yet as you command it so you are commanding separation between yourself and the whole

Universe! An example of such a reality is the belief that everyone—feminine structures in particular—should be thin. If you accept this reality and you are thin, then you become identified with that body, and you separate yourself. If you accept the reality and you are not thin, you become identified with that body, and you separate yourself. So whether you are thin or not thin, you are hooked in by the same beliefs.

You can see how having all these beliefs hooks you in to a mass consciousness. But how can you be hooked in and separated at the same time? You are separated from yourself! Since the mass consciousness is always about measuring yourself against another, you get into a state of defense. You become engaged, letting the opinions around you begin to matter, begin to be true. So you get into a state of justifying why an opinion is true or not true, rather than honoring that it's simply another dear brother's. You begin giving credibility and energy to different scenarios around you, and as you do that you begin to give yourself away to the scenarios, rather than just letting them pass by. This is what I call becoming engaged. You give your power away and suddenly the world is running you.

Emotion is a perceptional belief system that creates a judgment, a truth about oneself, taking pure consciousness, pure energy, and bringing it into a certain form: "I'm a good person," or, "I'm a bad person," or, "This is how the world works, and I can't change it." Once again, the funny part is that you as Creator Incarnate made these judgments into truth. So perhaps you say, "I'm fat, and I'm not worthy." And you see evidence in the world that others think this way. Then you say, "I'm fat, and I don't deserve anything." And from there you get involved in a cyclical cycle: "I'm fat, and I will always be fat. I will never deserve anything." And if you're thin, other false beliefs can attack from the mind level. You say, "I'm thin, so I should be happy. But I'm not happy. What's wrong with me?"

Do you see how this works? A set of beliefs soon becomes a belief system. One belief creates another, creates another, creates another, in a domino effect. Each belief creates more meanings, more meanings, more meanings, and defines you further. But the state of defining also creates a state of confinement. What about being male or female? You're taught that you must accept the mass consciousness beliefs about men and women. Take the beliefs that males are strong but cold, and females are weak but more loving. From that set of beliefs comes another rather old-fashioned belief that strong males must love sports, but feminine structures cannot. You must become more and more polarized from your true self to follow the belief system exactly. And it's tricky, because belief systems change all the time. Now feminine structures are almost <u>expected</u> to like sports, and some will try to like sports when they don't really have an interest. As we said, one belief may feel much more exuberant than another. It may feel better to think, "I am good enough," than to think, "I am not good enough." But although one thought feels better, both thoughts are still polarizing you. What if you simply said, "It just is"? The body just Is. The mind just Is.

Now you know that each of you has many perceptional identities. These have been created out of what you've perceived and experienced in the world, the guides you've had, your mother, father, sister, brother, etc., and those outside your monad. In fact, first separation from your higher levels occurred the moment you began to be identified with the world, when you began to let it dictate who you are. When you began to let the world become real, letting it run your life stream, the identification to a gender principle was presented and began to be created. Perceptional judgments are deities that are based in outside world events and activities, and it is what's going on outside of you that demands this be a good situation or a bad situation. You give the mind level a whole lot of energy to let it take charge and to let these external events become real. As your mind makes one perceptional judgment after another, you begin to define yourself through the world's perceptions, and your body slows down.

Belief is a phantom that the mind has made real that has nothing to do with You, the real You, the true You. Consider what happens when you take one certain scenario, experience, or one certain decision, and command it to be a part of you: "I am someone who makes $100,000 a year." When you do this, you are creating a "me"—a set of identifications and beliefs—rather than a being who is open to everything. When you create this "me," this identification, you automatically begin to close yourself off from everything new, whether it be positive or negative. These identifications can include such forms as a house, a car, a bank account, credit cards, or any material thing that the mass consciousness gives value and equates with self worth. These forms have been solidified over eons, and they have become real deities within your consciousness. You think you can't be happy without these trappings of happiness. Now let's be clear—there's nothing wrong with wanting to experience the very best. But what is the very best? That is something You decide. When you let the mass consciousness decide, that's where the forms begin to run you.

You may say, "We have to have beliefs! And without emotions, life would just be too boring, always the same." But I say that you have been run by the physical, mental, and emotional matrixes that make up the mass consciousness. Now you can live in the freedom beyond emotion which is letting everything be what it is. And how boring does that sound? But then if you're going to let everything be what it is, well, where do you fit into the planetary structure? The answer is that you fit in everywhere.

As you put nothing—no belief, no judgment, no emotion—into your life stream, you have everything. You also have your mind and your body—your best friends—with you. This is automatically going to change your outside world and your physical world. Now everything is starting to take back its power and take on its own life again just because you gave the go-ahead. You can start to question what is, and that is a whole new world. How many of you are taught not to question anything? Whether it be religious beliefs, whether it be nutrition, whether it be ideals of success; most dear brothers believe what they're taught. So what happens when you give yourself the go ahead to ask questions, to look at the world without the mind controlling you?

When you question the taught perceptional judgments and the emotions they cause, your life opens up. The questioning really doesn't have anything to do with the little you. The questions come from your higher levels. You're letting yourself open fully and completely, to flourish, evolve, and thrive, getting to have fun with yourself in this embodiment. So the questioning is really your natural state. Now you could be taking classes, reading books on spirituality, looking for something or some way to feel. Or you could be paying attention to that nudge you feel when you want to give yourself the go-ahead. And you can let the nudge begin to present in your world, letting your higher levels take care of the rest. Now you are playing with true guidance without creating a stronghold of emotions, identities or perceptions. You are not forcing the issues, or trying to make something happen that does not serve you. You are letting opportunities present on their own. Because even as you're letting things happen on their own, you can have complete and total freedom, complete divinity, complete laughter and excitement and enjoyment. You will find that you cannot wait to get up in the morning, or the evening, or whenever, to see what presents next.

Imagine in the course of your daily events you get a nudge from your higher levels: "I might like to learn Spanish." And some dear brothers tell you that scientists have proven it is very hard to learn a new language at your age. You still have that nudge, that mysterious calling to learn. Now at this point you might decide not to try out this new language, because it is too hard. Or you might become determined to learn Spanish no matter what the scientists say. But there is another way to look at the situation. What if you simply question all "wisdom" and begin learning? And what if you do this without a lot of hoping, without a lot of visualizing, or energy put into it? What if you put the energy into the learning? And what if you begin speaking Spanish without having a <u>purpose</u>, just because you wish to do it?

This is a good time to talk about the "Law of Attraction." We think and we create. The Law of Attraction is a universal principle, and it has served humanity for eons. The Law of Attraction says that what you contemplate is what you receive. It asks you to pick a certain finite focal point with the idea of attracting an object, a situation, a scenario into your life stream. Let's say you want a house, a car, a relationship, a child, or maybe you just want to get along with your family. Whatever it is, you set an intention and you begin to focus intensely on attracting it to your experience. This exercise literally throws your mind forward to create a specific picture of an outcome, a specific scenario. And you focus so intensely on bringing that into your life stream, you begin celebrating it before it arrives.

So when dear brothers began to examine the Law of Attraction, it was about coming to terms with having the ability to create, the ability to attract their wantings, their unwantings—literally having a say-so over their physical world. But then you grow beyond it as you're beginning to feel, sense, intuitively pick up on and be presented with new information. If you are in hyper-focus, hoping to attract something, you won't notice what is presenting right in front of you. These opportunities and options are presented from your higher levels, and this is also a universal principle. You begin to see, beyond simply believing it, that you don't have to force anything. You don't have to manifest anything. You simply show up at the right time. And somehow things have a way of working out without your intention. And along with your openness to walk through a new door as it presents will come a freedom you will cherish.

Your journey is continually taking on its own life. So you're going to make this agreement, or that agreement, while being able to enjoy everything from a neutrality state, and being able to enjoy all of the presences around you. Then you are completely free and wide open to everything else, because now you're going to be enjoying the dear ones that you're playing with. You are also enjoying them as the brilliance that they are and watching how your world takes on a whole new life. Once again, you're not trying to enjoy—enjoyment happens 24/7 naturally. And as it is happening, watch how completely exuberant and excited you become as you're giving the go-ahead in your life. You're letting yourself enjoy everything around you that's only going to continue to grow and open further.

The freedom from emotions is the beginning of being free of judgment. Your natural state is one of fluidity. You are not <u>trying</u> to be in a flow. Fluidity is being and becoming the flow. Your natural fluidity means letting everything around you take place, not needing to do anything with it, not needing the self-importance of the mind to change things, not needing to make things different. Because having to make a difference starts to create a conflicted state, and now you're going to become externally focused and internally critical. And then, you're going to attempt to stop or change these events, and you're going to become identified with them.

When you begin creating perceptional judgments of how things should be, how they are, how they are not, you're going to start to anchor these events into a reality. As you begin to anchor these beliefs in as reality there's no longer that fluidity. And now you're starting to create a blockage that affects your body vehicle. It also affects your clarity. This belief system starts to create a reality and identification of who you are and where you're at. The worst part is that once you begin to split yourself off from your Creator essence, everything around you begins to shut down.

Have you ever been around a dear brother who wants to talk about politics or religion, two subjects that can create walls a million miles high? This is someone who has become dedicated to a cause, and can't seem to think about anything else. Because in truth, nothing else really exists for him. His mind will accept no alternatives to his ideals. Think of the rigidity in his body vehicle, in the way he raises his voice, his intensity. He has <u>become</u> the cause, so identified with it that the two cannot be separated. And it's really quite comical to see other dear ones as they react to him, to agree or disagree. Then <u>they</u> become their own cause. This sometimes even happens to dear ones who have no interest in either subject!

Remember that the mind can be a brilliant tool and friend, but you must always be ready to question what it tells you. For example, harsh self-judgments can start to affect your pancreas, your insulin levels, your sugar levels. So your sugar levels are high. And that's where the mind really starts to go against you. It identifies itself with your father's, father's, father's, father who left the planet with pancreatic cancer at age 38. You certainly wouldn't choose to command that as a reality for yourself, would you? But you were taught that you have no power over your genetics. So, now your mind says you have only a couple of choices: If you are going to identify yourself with your genetics, you might as well have as much fun as you can now because at age 38 you'll be leaving the planet. Or you could never do anything for fear that if you do you will be leaving the planet at 38. Either way is a prison.

When you begin to question and explore what truly is, you'll find that all of the accepted and assumed judgments become suspect. You begin to see that it was truly your great-great grandfather's journey, and not yours. That life journey was just the way that he accepted it had to be. So now you ask yourself, "Who am I, and where am I?" This is the where a volcano of that energy called emotion begins to release. Don't forget what is happening now. You are becoming the real You, re-contemplating living beyond the heaviness and taught behavioral mannerisms that are no longer in charge. Once the emotions that have been running your life have been exposed, they will begin to dissolve.

You begin to see your manifest levels, the levels that present many different opportunities for you. Can you believe it when an opportunity presents for you and you actually take it? I've seen this so many times, when a job promotion comes out of nowhere for a dear brother. Or someone wants to start a business and the connections just seem to appear. "Wow!" you say. "What just happened?" The opportunity that came your way was much more than what you were taught would be possible. But now the mind can't deny it because it's right there before you.

Now you may be getting a little bit uncomfortable because there's really so much more that you can play with in your life that you haven't noticed until now. Let's examine this a bit further. Maybe three dear brothers came into your life stream today. You may not be sure you can trust them yet, so let's just let it be. Don't be involved with where your relationships go, but simply wait and see. And watch what happens for you. In time, two of them will disappear from your life just like that. But the other one came into your life to stay.

Where did you learn that you had to tell lies to yourself or someone else in order to make things happen? When were you taught that you had to work hard for everything? Do you remember how you were taught that the whole world was against you? Do you remember being told that you would have to struggle to survive, that achievement came at a steep price? Those were the old perceptional judgments that you made, and all of the emotion around them that kept you running and controlled your whole life. Now are you tired of running, of letting the old perceptional judgments, presumptions and emotions run your life? Then say, "Show me what is possible higher levels. You are in command."

The results are truly remarkable. I have seen dear ones without college educations become the CEOs of corporations. "Wow, how could this ever be possible?" you ask. Well, they started to take a look at what could be possible. Because they gave themselves the chance, opportunities presented, everything presented right there for them. Are you starting to understand this a little bit? It's so simple, so easy, yet so often denied.

So maybe what you were taught wasn't quite accurate. Your father told you that life isn't fair. Maybe what your father told you is what his father and his grandfather told him. And because it is not quite accurate, you wonder about all the other things he taught you. What is the truth? Who are you really? Where do you fit? Where do you stand? By being an offspring, must you embody all the heavy responsibilities of the past?

When you begin to question what is, opportunities can start presenting. Wow, here comes another opportunity. Is this starting to feel a little bit familiar to you now? Look at all this energy, all these beliefs that you were taught and that you bought into. Of course, that wasn't your fault. If you didn't buy into the whole system, that proved there was something wrong with you. You would have been disciplined, lacerated and otherwise if you didn't believe in the system. But all these behaviors that you've been observing and exhibiting really have not been feeling too good, have they? Now when you take a look at the mass consciousness and explore its ideals, you see why the mind and emotions can no longer be in charge. Now what else is there to be played with? What else is there to be explored? What else is possible? Are you feeling more neutral within now? Are you ready for something new? Are you ready to fully embrace all of You?

You may be feeling a little bit uncomfortable because of the awakening of your natural state. Now you are playing with a whole new realm of what can be. You have a beautiful, beautiful feeling, a presence that you don't recognize, you haven't ever felt this way before. It goes against what the mind was taught. You may find that it feels like love. It feels a little bit familiar, even though it must have been eons since you felt this way. There are no lows, there are no highs, and the feeling is constant.

Could you live in a world where there's nothing you have to pretend to be or not be? This is the dream of a lifetime that you wouldn't even give yourself permission to dream. You were taught with great emotion and drama that you had to grow up, go to school, find a career, get engaged, get married, and have offspring. Then your life would basically be over except for going through the repetition of providing. And you watched this whole cycle, watched your mom, your dad; you saw all of the family dynamics. And you started down this path yourself.

I ask you to take heed of everyone else's journey, and now go beyond it. What if you don't try to fix their issues any longer, or try to fix your issues? What if you don't try to figure out why you attracted them into your lifestream? Why not simply become free from carrying them, from becoming identified with what's going on in their lifestreams? For so long it has been the mind's job to take care of them. It has been the mind's job to create self-importance, trying to make everything around you okay, to make everyone else happy. Are you now starting to realize that the more you attempt to do for these dear ones the more they keep repeating themselves? They keep getting caught up in the same mental information. They keep getting caught up in the same behavioral mannerisms. They keep referring back to the same old paradigms, thought forms, identifications, emotions. They are like people lost in a forest and going in circles. They keep referring back to the old information of the mind and beliefs. What you can do is love them so dearly, guiding them through the old and bringing them into the truth of who they are. They are beginning to recognize that their behavior really hasn't been serving them or anyone else, and the old perceptions are not working for them any longer. Their guidance realms are wanting to walk them through.

I question how many are acting a certain way because they were taught to act that way, rather than because that's who they truly are? When they get up in the morning and they're going to make the coffee, and beginning to get ready for work, going to work, do they have smiles on their faces? And are those smiles real, or do they smile even though they're mourning inside? Let's ask the mourning, "What are you about?" And what's the answer? You may be doing all the right things but still feel unfulfilled. What is that void? What is that hole in your complete fulfillment? What seems to be missing?

All your perceptional identities and judgments and emotions that you have put into this one certain situation that you've been so identified with aren't giving you the fulfillment you're asking for. You've seen dear ones walking on the perceptionally less fortunate side with a genuine smile on their faces. You've seen clerks in convenience stores or department stores with that brilliant gleam of joy in their eyes. You've seen garbage collectors with that gleam. Why do they have it?

Let's explore You further. Give yourself the go-ahead, permission to be free from emotions. Let the emotion begin to drain out of you. Give yourself the go-ahead to question. Now let's start playing with the elemental levels around you. Can you see and feel the changes taking place around you? Can you feel the openness and expansion around you? Are you starting to feel more comforted? Can you feel that maybe, just possibly you're not alone in this Universe, or even in a body on a planet? Can you feel the changes taking place in the room? Even in the body you're in? In a certain sense, so much is coming to you from your expanded states, so much more is being provided for, just because you decided to give yourself a chance.

Can you believe that you just felt—really felt—your body? And as you're exploring this feeling, watch how everything begins to restore itself. Now all of the polyps in your colon have just flushed through, and the body is beginning to detoxify itself of debris. Now you can let all of the colorful memories that you've been having in your dream states, even your waking states, be complete. Now a whole different career that you can actually enjoy, actually love, may begin to present. And the abundance can begin to come in—more than you could ever have dreamed of or imagined. Now you're in a whole new world.

Suddenly you're getting another promotion, or you've moved into something completely new. How could this be happening? Everything in your life stream, abundance and otherwise, is taking care of itself. "So what do I do?" asks the mind. And you realize it has nothing to do. These old patterns, these old perceptional judgments, emotions, now they seem so foreign to you. They really have nothing to do with you anymore. You were presented with all of these colorful beliefs and thoughts, like having a God poised above you with a big giant stick, attempting out of great love to beat you into a kind of submission, forcing you to be something different from your true self rather than complementing it. Now you can feel these old cellular memories dissolving on every level.

"Do you mean I can actually have a marriage without discontent, or a conflict, or a disconnect?" you ask. "Do you mean I don't even have to have an opinion? Can I just simply be in my natural state? Do you mean I can just simply continue to play with who I am, and have a complement right there beside me, someone who can do the same, two hearts coming together?" You don't have to have a domination approach based in the emotion of the male being this, the feminine structure being that. "Show me," you say.

Then here comes the most brilliant pearl, the most brilliant jewel, the most brilliant diamond. And you are going to walk together side by side. Are your eyes filling with tears of relief and love? This is what I have been feeling since I met my bride—not emotion, not judgment, not the combustible energy that's just waiting to roar and find a target to blame. Only a gift of love. What a brilliant blessing it is for the whole Universe and your Creator levels to offer this communion with a dear one, a complete communion of the heart, a complete dance together.

What I find so colorful, so inspiring, is that the heart's being open is definitely <u>not</u> about emotion. Emotion is all about control. The heart is all about love. It's about your own divine essence coming to the forefront. It somehow feels familiar but so scary to the mind level, to an egoic structure. Do you keep having these odd dreams of two hearts becoming one? Two cyclical rings becoming one—what does that mean? Could it be that you're becoming one together in the emanation that you're presenting completely from the heart to this exponential world? There are no highs or lows. You are just the love that continues to grow and expand every moment as Creator Incarnate, continuing to embody the brilliant exquisiteness beyond time. It is You emanating You.

And you watch so many of these dear brothers around you acting out all over the place. Some will be wanting what you have. Some are very, very jealous because although they've followed all the rules to a "T" in their marriages, the rules haven't worked for them. And those marriages become about having an outburst here, an outburst there, arguing, trying to dominate, trying to get a point across, just like they thought they were supposed to. Because it's taught that you have to throw a giant temper tantrum to be noticed. And all along, they could have just been enjoying each other's essence, being the presence, and the love that they are and share.

Don't be surprised that dear ones are coming to you. Not to mimic your life, but to find some assistance to be able to wake up—to dissolve all of this stuff that was taught, including the emotion of how humanity is "supposed" to behave. And now watch as these same dear ones are starting to step into their own. Now watch marriages completing, marriages opening and flourishing again. You see dear ones becoming free of emotion and dissolving old behavioral mannerisms they weren't even aware they were acting out and mimicking.

This is what happens to a being who is free of judgment states. This is what happens when you're letting the journey be the destination, when you start to let go and see emotion for what it is. This is also what happens when you begin to question yourself, and question your behavioral mannerisms. You are awakening into freedom from density, freedom from conflict, freedom from emotion. You begin to know what it's like to be free from emotional relationships, from the topsy-turvy, back and forth, conflict-after-conflict, "I'm right, you're wrong," and "You're right, I'm wrong" relationships. This is freedom from feeling and acting out emotions. It is the real You starting to feel your presence.

This is both a great gift and a challenge. I know that most dear brothers will move back and forth between the mind and the higher levels, especially as they become accustomed to living without emotion. Changing over means switching back from the physical to your higher levels; it is changing direction, welcoming in your higher levels as different scenarios are playing out. Going from the mind level back through

the heart level once again, you bring your consciousness right back to the heart and beyond the mind. It is
truly a dancing back and forth.

Challenge is brilliant. Re-contemplation is brilliant. So start to challenge your behavior, and what you
think you know as well. You say, "I want to know the
truth of All That Is." Now give yourself the go-ahead
to know that truth. And as you are moving into your
own presence, the presence of divinity, the presence
of oneness, in communion with All That Is, you are
free to express the divinity that you are. As you are free
to express your divinity, it is your own presence you
are feeling right now. It is your heart that you're feeling, rather than the mind that says, "I think I should, I
ought, I must, I want, I need."

Freedom is a state of expansion, clarity, wide openness, where nothing but nothing has power over you.
It is your natural state. You know that to have a belief
is to create a wall. Living beyond beliefs means living
in a state of complete freedom. You allow yourself to
be expanded throughout every particle of consciousness—cellular, atomic, subatomic. Freeing yourself
of beliefs is letting the outside world be the outside
world, giving power to no thing, no object, no other
dear brother on the planet, no scenario, no belief, no
identification, no gender. It is truly to embody and
embrace All That Is, letting the world open. You let
yourself dance in the world, let the days take care of
the days, let yourself be alive to everything that is presenting. By living beyond beliefs, you are setting your
mind free, your body free, stepping into true mastery
of love, and availability of the Universe.

MEDITATION ON TRUE RELATIONSHIPS

You may wish to have someone read this meditation to you or record yourself reading it so you can follow along easily. Also, you can do these meditations with or without closing your eyes and over time you may experience that there is no need to close your eyes at all.

As you bring your consciousness back through the
palm of your hand
all the way up your wrist
through your forearm
your upper arm
through your neck
through your shoulders
through the other upper arm
through the lower arm
through the wrist
through the hand
bringing your palms together about 5 inches apart
from each other
let's feel the presence of you
streaming through the body principle at this time
the warmth
the tingling

the fruition
the fluidity
the expansion
the openness
and take your palms and slide them across each other
and bring your left hand onto your chest
and your right hand out towards the world
and just relaxing
letting the energy run through your body principle
feeling the presence of you
which is life beyond action and reaction
it's a life completely of being fully embodied
as the presence of divinity of which you are
no longer having idle buttons of chit chat
perceptional judgments
life of emotions
or having the world run you
because you're fully, truly, completely opening up
and expanding through this world
being in the world
but not of it

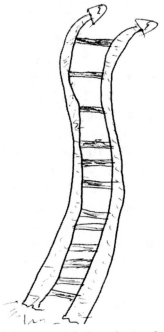

On this DNA strand notice the cracks in the telomere, the end caps. Cracking and chipping of the telomere causes aging. This damage to the telomere is caused by going against your true self.

Chapter 4

REBUILDING YOUR DNA AND RAISING YOUR VIBRATORY STRUCTURES

We've spoken about your ability to enjoy the most brilliant relationships by losing belief, emotion and judgment, by living in a world where the mind does not control you, but functions with you as your friend. In this chapter we'll talk about letting your body become your friend. I call this "letting the body be the body." You have the ability to rebuild your DNA, to raise your vibratory levels, and to live in optimum health and well-being; if only you will begin treating the body as the dear friend it is. Learning to treat the body as your friend has everything to do with letting go of belief and emotion, and becoming disengaged from the mass consciousness.

How do beliefs and emotions work on the body? They affect the body on a cellular level while affecting your vibratory levels as well. Think of your cellular structures as a composition of cells that are making up one physical format of consciousness. It is these cellular structures your body has been playing with throughout your whole life stream. For example, there are billions of particles of consciousness that make up your bones, your muscles, your tendons, or your skin. Billions more particles take the form of a certain organ, such as your liver, gall bladder, pineal and pituitary glands, colon, or your stomach. And let's not forget the billions of particles that make up your brain.

Through its cellular atomic and subatomic structures the body has taken on and brought into itself many different resonances and particles of perceptional identities. When an identity is created the atomic and subatomic particles begin to fluctuate, and function in a whole different way. The result of the identifications that you create affects the functionability of your physicality, begins the aging process and causes the breakdown of your body vehicle.

You see, the brain is your filter for all of the attributes of this world. It also arranges and runs the chemical formats for the rest of the organs of your physicality. Looking into the brain from the top down, it is the scanner and weaver of consciousness. It is in charge of running the physical streams, the central nervous system, the autonomic nervous system, the parasympathetic nervous system, and a host of other functions. And what about its relatively <u>unaccessed</u> abilities, such as stepping through many different doorways or stepping into altered realms? The brain is designed to perform its functions when it is wide awake and fully alert. And because all of the brain's chemical processes are affected by your beliefs, emotions and judgments, sometimes the brain performs better than other times. Sometimes the brain is more conscious—more awake—than at other times. In turn, your brain's chemical processes affect your body's cellular and vibratory levels.

Your body's vibratory levels are not spoken of as often as your cellular structures, but they have everything to do with how your body functions. Megahertz is the measurable level of the speed at which your body is vibrating. As changes take place in your physicality, your vibratory levels can slow down or speed up dramatically. Much of humanity is vibrating at around 48,000 megahertz per second. When the body is vibrating at only 48,000 megahertz per second, the cerebral cortex of the brain opens up to allow thought forms to enter the physicality. The body vibrates slower, while particles of thoughts, particles of perceptional beliefs and judgments come in to create stagnation and heaviness. That begins to slow down your vibratory structure, creating chaos and disruption in both the body and the mind.

The body vehicle is the deity of consciousness you are using and residing in at this moment in time to express your own uniquedness. This vehicle is something like a piece of machinery when left alone. When you leave the body alone, you are completely and totally expressing and expanding beyond and through it. This allows the body vehicle to begin rewriting itself, regenerating itself beyond the monadic make-up, the genetic make-up, the DNA make-up. It merely wants to be honored with what it asks for. Please remember, the body loves to communicate with you, to be heard, to be experienced. In fact, the body wants nothing more than to create a relationship with you.

But the kind of relationship you create is important. My body level is a beautiful, beautiful tool. But I am not my body, and it is not me. The body is my friend, not my master. Take a look at yourself and the dear ones around you: Can you say the same? Or do you identify too much with your physicality? This is when the body and the mind-levels take control. And when the little "me" takes control, the body begins to suffer big time.

For example, as you join into a monad, a soul group, you begin to take on certain physical traits that have become a genetic format. The genetic format is a state that assumes you're going to have certain actions and reactions through your physical conduit. And for eons this genetic format has been creating a breakdown of the physical portal. In the clear state of your body now, genetics no longer has the same power to effect a breakdown of your body vehicle. But listen to what your <u>mind</u> says about genetics.

Genetics involves a certain encodement, a certain repetitiveness through generations. It's a very solidified form and format that has created a chain reaction through the centuries. Your genetics determines what your hair or skin shade will be. The scientists tell you that the way you age has to do with your genetics. But there are also a lot of thought particles surrounding the ideals of genetics, a lot of mass consciousness beliefs associated with genetic identities, a lot of beliefs about aging itself, and this leads to further encodements. The aging of a physicality is a response to <u>all</u> of these embodied encodements. The physicality receives the message that creates a constant chain reaction through your body vehicle. So involvement in mass consciousness beliefs creates a stronger encodement than the actual genetics.

When you let the body be the body, organ levels function brilliantly, and the body recreates and regenerates itself. When your organ levels become identified with experiential realms, when you are hijacked into identities outside of yourself, this begins to create conflict after conflict with your body. And conflict brings judgment after judgment that gets presented and projected on to your organ levels, slowing down your body principle. Do you remember when I spoke about the way harsh self judgments affect the pancreas? Let's say that you experience those same harsh judgments for years on end. As time passes, your organs lose their ability to withstand the conflict. The pancreas begins to fail. Of course, it would be easier to blame the failure of the pancreas on genetics. As all of these primitive, little "me" identifications are continuing to be cleared out and disengaged from this world, it allows for the cellular structures to re-arise, speeding up their vibrational frequencies. And as the vibratory levels of the body vehicle are speeding up even further, all of these old archaic identities begin to break down further as well.

By beginning to explore and question, you start to be presented with your physicality as a live deity, a live consciousness. You become aware of the atomic structures—and the subatomic structures—becoming disengaged from the dense matter principle. The absence of emotion allows you to find the true complete expression of your body vehicle. The physicality now becomes more than a tool, a toy, an apparatus of enjoyment. It becomes the expression of You and the presence that You are. For the body principle is a presence of its own. It has immense reserves of strength and is capable of so much more than we acknowledge.

As you allow the body to be the body, watch how quickly it will regenerate itself, rebuild itself, create changes to further complement you. This is what is within the body vehicle, from appearance to optimum health and vitality, to functionability. All you must do is allow the body to show you its own capabilities of fruition and honoring. It only wants to be acknowledged as the brilliant gift that it is, by being enjoyed and allowed to function.

And the beauty is, you can change everything right now! What causes the breakdown of the DNA? It is caused by what you <u>believe</u> you must do to be healthy, whole, and complete. It is caused by what you believe you must do to be, or at least <u>appear</u> to be, important. It is caused by what you believe you need to do to survive in a body on a planet. But now you're letting all of that be dissolved. When you examine your body vehicle, is it feeling light? Or is it feeling heavy? Right now, let's bind all the density out of your body principle, to allow it to come back to life.

Telomeres are the end caps of your DNA, which are also called the youth and vitality chromosomes. With every perceptional belief that you are creating or buying into, the telomere develops chips or cracks, and begins breaking down. In the aging process, the telomere chips away, and this starts to create the breakdown of the physicality. The body begins to shut itself down, which is called being "over the hill," or some such metaphor. The funny thing is that all these assumptions that go along with the chipping away of the telomere really help create a shutdown in the body principle. Due to being very asleep and listening to accepted beliefs, humanity keeps making assumptions about what is going to happen to the body, and when it's going to happen. But what if you started to examine your DNA right now? Once you see the truth, you can begin to reverse the process. So right now, let's allow the telomere to begin rebuilding itself.

One way to reverse the aging process is to tune in to an area and start to re-contemplate and re-question how it feels. You start to know what ailments or problems are humanity-made rather than body-made. Notice the perceptional beliefs created by the mind that says, "This is definitely going to happen to me, and this is <u>when</u> it's going to happen." When you simply begin to question the belief, that's when changes start to happen. Those changes have to do with quantum physics—they are changes that occur at the particle level. When you start to make a different decision, you have the total complete say so and go-ahead to let things be different. You can be in a full complete wide open state, and that's where you bypass time and the aging process.

When you begin to question the way your body vehicle functions—to question everything for that matter—vibratory levels are no longer locked into one certain format or another. You're able to go beyond the general level of functioning, to unlock your body vehicle from a lower level of vibratory frequency. By doing that, you allow the whole body to be unhooked and free to recreate itself. This automatically speeds up the vibratory levels even further. Every question you ask yourself begins to create openings and changes in these vibratory levels.

Brain chemistry refers to the chemical structures of the brain that react to what's going on around you. The chemical balance is always changing, as the body and mind are still so identified with this world and this planetary structure. When the little "me" takes over, the brain is infused with so many harmful chemicals. The mind that says, "I think, I should, I ought, I must," in its impulsive states creates this infusion. This in turn creates an unregulated state of the body, where body and brain no longer function together.

As you move into the body principle, becoming comfortable in the body, you open up these chemistries to be heightened, you move toward a full complete embodied state of consciousness within the physical. This will allow for so much more activity and accessibility through your body principle. And when you get to a heightened state of brain levels, all systems are functioning in alignment to further open you and let you be so much more open. This enables you to move so far beyond your old identities in this world. In this heightened state, you have a heightened accessibility to off planet support. You become aware that this whole Universe moves together as One. You understand that rather than just keeping your head down looking into this world, you can be aware of what is going on across the galaxies. By marrying with your higher levels, you function at your optimum level.

When you marry your higher and lower levels, you enter a neutrality state. Within this state you can change your brain chemistries to complement the body vehicle, creating a whole new chemical programming. This leads to a whole new set of chemical reactions within the brain as it begins to restabilize. As your higher levels become more involved, the chemistries of the brain begin to re-level themselves until serotonin and melatonin re-connect and complement each other. As you're letting yourself be open, the brain chemistries can realign, and your brain will begin creating new chemical formulas. These formulas are allowing you to access the brain's pleasure centers to release a whole different level of endorphins. Brain chemistry can once again give your body stability, a centeredness, along with clarity. Imagine the processability of chemicals opening, opening, beginning to generate new chemicals, creating new chemical balances. Do you see how this allows you to fully and completely enjoy the body principle and its innate abilities? And do you see that those abilities are so much more accessible when you're letting the body take on its own life?

Let me explain a bit: Let's say my body presents that it's time to detoxify. It needs to spend some time processing. "Okay," I say, "time to detoxify. Body, go ahead and take care of it. Thanks." And then I go on with my day, and don't give it another thought. Now how can that work? It works because my body is my friend, it's going to remain, always, always, in a constant state of dialogue, communion, and communication as long as I'm open to it. This is what I mean by letting the body be the body—let the body take care of itself. Sure enough, sometimes the body will create what I call a "perceptional virus". I say "perceptional" because there is nothing real about it.

While it might look like a virus to someone else, the body is just flushing itself through. The next thing I know the phone rings, and I get back to work again, assisting a dear brother. And the body's more vibrant than ever, wide awake and fully alert and having a blast; it is my companion. Everything is in optimum health and well-being. When I hang up the phone, guess what happens? The body starts flushing itself again as it needs to. I'm dancing with it, and then the phone rings again and I'm off. Have you noticed that your body might feel weak and tired at one point in the day, and later you find yourself going out to dinner, and still later you go home and the body continues to detoxify? You didn't have to be "sick" to allow the body to right itself, you simply got your mind out of the way. The body has this brilliant consciousness. So once again, it's not about controlling the body, but about letting it be.

Playing with the consciousness of food and all of the belief systems built around it is another great example of the mind getting in the way. Food is made to be put into the body vehicle, giving it sustenance to recreate itself. Whether it be vegetables, or proteins, or any of the other diverse elements of culinary enjoyment, when partaken without judgment, the food does its job and passes right through the body vehicle.

And you know this to be true because there was a time before you were taught what food does, what grains do, what fibers do, what flour does and doesn't do. Before any of that was taught, you were completely wide open to everything. You were allowing your body to decide what it enjoyed. You let everything in this whole Universe take care of itself and you were just here to enjoy.

Then you started to be taught all about food through the chain of command—first the parents, and then the scholastic systems, followed by the food charts, the nutritionists, then the TV shows and magazines. All of this "educating" served a brilliant purpose to begin with, but it grew out of control. Remember that the mind level is always trying to protect you, but it gets carried away. Now I ask you, whatever gave this piece of chocolate cake so much power in the first place? You've grown to think there is something so bad about cake, the only time you can allow yourself to have it is when there is a celebration at hand or when your mind level is feeling depressed. Is that the only time that you can have something of sweetness for enjoyment? Now what would happen if you let yourself have the cake just because you enjoyed it? Isn't it possible that the judgment you have about eating it is worse for your body than the cake itself? Isn't it just possible that if you didn't involve your emotions, your body would simply enjoy the cake and let it go?

Whether it be natural or processed, "healthy" or "unhealthy", whether it comes from McDonald's or an elegant gourmet restaurant, you have to look at food for what it is. The key is to eat from a state of neutrality, from a state of enjoyment, to consume for enjoyment without judgment. You may have a carrot or a piece of chocolate cake, a pear or a giant hamburger. Which is better? Which is healthier? When you begin to explore what's healthy about these foods, how many beliefs come up? What if you could eat from a state of total neutrality? You would also be letting your body become the judge of what it wants.

Now let's look at this from a different perspective: Nutrient elements are what the body is asking for as a boost, as a jump start. These nutrient elements allow the body vehicle to continue to flourish, to regenerate, rebuild, and amplify. They also give the body a job to do, as it wants nothing more than to be able to enjoy these elements; taking what's necessary to maintain optimum health, wellness and homeostasis, discarding the rest.

You only need nutrient elements to a certain degree. They complement the body as it's restabilizing, and then when you start to reawaken within the body principle the body starts living off itself. That's where food is no longer a necessity, but taken more for enjoyment. This has to do with your vibratory levels. For example, for the masses of humanity who are arising, their vibrations range between 48,000 and 76,000 megahertz per second. They require more sustenance daily. Once your body begins vibrating at around 86,000 megahertz per second or more, it requires very little sustenance. And when you reach 150,000 megahertz per second, your body will no longer become hungry. Your body will no longer require any sort of elements, because it will be able to continually regenerate itself. The point is, humanity has so many beliefs about food elements and places so much importance on food. But food is just that. It is not love, it is not success, and it is not a substitute for those things.

By looking at food this way, you are not getting hooked back into the mass consciousness. You are getting <u>unhooked</u>. And standing right here you can now see how the world is changing around you. Like right now, can you feel the energy, the vibratory levels changing in your own physicality? This change in vibratory frequency is rewriting the atomic, subatomic particles, rewriting the functionability of the pancreas, the abdomen, down to the gastric juices.

What we're doing by welcoming in the presence of You is giving up on hoping, trusting, and believing. Because of the essences emanating from your physical vehicle, you're already changing over the vibratory structures of your physical body level and your environment. Going further, you're also changing the encodements of consciousness and your genetic makeup, the genetic format, the DNA format. Here's an experiment you can use to assist you in understanding: You say, "Okay body; it's time to vibrate faster." And wow! Your body vibrates faster.

In beginning to raise your vibratory levels let's give your body permission, as we're starting to play in a realm that seems a little bit unsafe for the mind, a little bit uncomfortable, a little bit different than everything you've ever been taught. Let's give yourself permission to feel your essence through the physical, start to tune into what may be or may not be possible. Let's start to give yourself permission beyond creating a belief.

"Show me what's possible here," you say to your higher levels. Can you feel changes taking place in your body?

Let's pick a finite spot on your body that is very much a predominant focus for you, a place that you're more apt to be connected with than another. It may be your stomach that tends to ache at times. Or it could be the back of your neck where tensions build up. Let's make it on the chest, the forearm, the biceps. I may have uncomfortability in my colon, so let's put it on the colon. Try putting a a cog or a switch right there. So when everything's been built up in your body, you can hit the switch. Can you feel that ache begin to subside? The tightness beginning to loosen?

Now pick a spot on your lower neck or upper back, and let's put this metaphorical switch on it. Let's give the body the go-ahead: "Okay, it's time to dissolve the density, time to speed up the body principle." Can you feel the body beginning to change, beginning to release all the tensions, the stresses, the thought forms, all your conflicted perceptions and beliefs beginning to release? Now can you feel the consciousness in the room? Can you feel the openness? Or, for some, can you feel the density? Now ask yourself, "Could I change it without saying a word?"

Density is the cause of the continual slowing down of your vibratory levels. And the core essence of density is judgment. The cerebral cortex at the back of the brain lets you go through a clearing stage when the body vibrates at 68,000 megahertz per second. When you begin to welcome in your essence, everything becomes clearer as your vibratory levels speed up. All becomes and feels much more familiar and now more available and clear for you. As you now give permission, watch your vibratory structures continue to rise. And once you get up to 85,000 megahertz, you have reached a plateau because you cannot go back to a slower way of being. The numbers and megahertz only continue to rise as you have now given yourself and your body the permission to be awake and to stay awake as Creator essence emanating through the physicality. You may reach 100,000 megahertz, even 185,000 megahertz.

I can tell you that just by walking into a room my own presence is changing the vibratory structures and the vibratory levels. That's not an egoic statement. It is true for you as well; it's your natural state of innate abilities that are emanating. Have you had the chance to notice how all the dear brothers around you begin to open? Of course, some feel more activated than others. Out of great love, all of them are inviting you in to fully and completely assist them to break down these structures. As you do this, you are also assisting them to raise their own vibratory levels quite naturally. That gets you wondering, "What would happen if I raised the vibratory structures in this room by putting a metaphoric knob or cog on the wall to turn it up?" And just like that, you're changing over the vibratory levels in the room.

This is an ability that you have already, but don't always recognize. Even right now as we're playing in this book, if you turn up the vibratory structures in your home, watch how quickly everyone reaches a much more harmonious state. Not without some acting out, some emotional outbursts, but these are just combustible energies that have been locked into the physical, that the dear brothers are no longer wanting. The energies are releasing, saying, "Pop, pop, pop, pop, pop!" They're coming up and out to be permanently dissolved.

Let's start to challenge the everyday ideas a little bit. So, I'm going to set it forward that just maybe, without being bamboozled, without being tricked or going down a primrose path, that things could actually change for you, all the way to your mental surroundings. So let's put that knob on the wall, and turn up the vibratory principle. Let's turn it up. And at the same time, let's watch what happens in your body due to the increased vibration in your surroundings. Go ahead and turn it up, without moving a muscle, without visualizing. Just command it up the scale.

Now let's start to give the room the go-ahead. "Okay, it's time to speed up the vibratory structures." Can you get a sense of things beginning to move, to amplify? Can you start to feel a difference in the room? Now watch what begins to happen around you, just out of curiosity, out of playing with your own abilities and beginning to become comfortable with them. Notice how you're beginning to become comfortable without shutting yourself down on what's possible or impossible. Let's continue to explore. Let's just let the world be what it is. And give yourself a chance. Give yourself the opportunity, the freedom, the space to start taking little glimpses through peepholes in the Universe, if you will. Start to explore yourself, to explore what may or could be possible, rather than becoming a victim of what you've been taught.

You felt different before, and you didn't like it. You certainly didn't want to stand out, or look different, or take the chance that you might seem odd. What if you were wrong? What if you made a mistake? What would you become? What would others think? How would they judge you? These are the questions the mind asked. Now you are playing with being wide open and letting your vibratory structures be more vibrant than ever. As you're doing that, watch how everything in your outside world mirrors your inside world. As you've been thinking about trying to fit in, you can feel how everything slows down, and how you're already feeling physically tired, worn out, exhausted. That's not natural. That's not your body, and that's not You. Then you stop trying. Can you feel the relief and the lightness throughout your being because you can actually be yourself again?

I am not suggesting that there may not be some discomfort at times. Let's say you have diabetes as a symptom. And you say to the body, "Let's turn up the pancreas." Okay, done deal. Now let's not be afraid of what happens. Of course your body is going to detoxify. Of course your body is going to flush through everything that it's ever experienced that was the original cause of your symptoms. There may be pain. Then again, what is pain but a state of mind? You fear pain, but how often do you see it for what it is? If it is a state of mind, can you just let it go?

You have held onto experiences and identified with them. For some of you that has been more on purpose than for others; some want to hold onto their anger, or pain, or whatever it may be. Being controlled by emotion was a lot more routine than being in one's own divinity. At least you knew where you stood with emotion. But now, we are taking it one exciting step further. Can you feel the pancreas changing? If need be, put your hands right there. Feel the buzzing going on through your physical. This is your molecular structure literally changing and beginning to rebuild.

And as we're exploring your innate abilities, let's not just play with the organs—how dull, boring, and uninteresting that would be! Let's watch what's going on with all the dear brothers around you. These events are not presenting by accident, but to dissolve control, arise beyond it and no longer be a slave to rules or taught behaviors that no longer work. You are freeing yourself from the slavery of the mind, and much more. You are escaping from the confinement of what is thought to be possible and not possible in this world. And when you are free, watch what begins to happen.

You're letting yourself soar beyond the planetary structures, beyond the physical, through the physical, and not denying it This gives the body vehicle complete freedom, complete divinity, gives it back its abilities to do what it does best—re-creating optimum health and well-being. I can promise you that you wanted the opportunity to wake up from the karmic grid system that kept you in a cyclical cycle of repetition. You would get to this certain point where you could re-contemplate your journey and decide if you wanted to continue on or step out of the body. What a brilliant window of opportunity you created! You allowed yourself to remember who You are and why You are here, as well as where you could go throughout your life stream and begin to fully and truly live and express the divinity that You are on your uniqued journey.

Now you've begun to step it up. You don't have to step out of the physicality. So you've given the body permission simply by creating a cog, a switch. It still comes back down to the fact that you have given the body permission to be the body. Why not play with turning up your own physical vibratory principle? Wow! Are you beginning to feel more exuberant than ever? As you're still coming into your own fluidity can you feel it within every particle of your physicality? What you're really tuning into is the speeding up and complete purification of your cells, your very molecules.

Please don't be alarmed when you're performing this little exercise if you suddenly have to go to the restroom. You may actually have all the symptoms of a virus; once again, it's that old perceptional virus. I can promise you, it's not really a virus at all. It's the removal of all the toxicities that have kept your body vibrating at that one certain speed. But then, done deal. Those toxicities are flushed out, never to return. What I love so much is that this perceptional virus is gone in moments as it's given no power.

You are giving the power back to the physical. And as you give power back to the physical to handle the physical, you're giving yourself back to your own divine abilities. There's nothing to be afraid of except what you were taught. And I know how many of you are saying, "I was taught to be afraid of myself. I was taught not to look outside of our belief systems. I was taught not to go beyond the biblical encodements.

I was taught it was not okay for me to feel the way that I feel." But why? Whoever said that because your father's, father's, father's, father was Lutheran, you've got to be Lutheran? It doesn't matter what you want or how you feel, it's just what you have to be. Have you ever wondered why certain illnesses and diseases run in families? You may assume that it is only because of the genetic encodements, the genetic format of your soul group. But this arises from a state of assumptions. It's these assumptive behaviors, these sleep-walking behaviors that break down your DNA. Judgment, confinement and separation cause the breakdown of your body and clarity as well as your DNA. Can you imagine what your life would be like if you let yourself be free to look at the world from an open clarity state?

You kept searching for answers. "What is it?" you asked. "What do I need?" You kept looking. Was it the advancement; was it the freedom from being sentenced to everyone else's perceptions, and from everyone else's identifications, i.e., the mass consciousness? You knew that answer existed somewhere. And then you find that all along the answer has been <u>You</u>, your own brilliant creation. And what happens now that you have the answer? Can you feel your wholeness returning? Some are going to feel that total urgency dissolve. It's as though you've filled the void you've felt with these answers, with levels of questions that you have been seeking answers for, some conscious, some unconscious. For some, there won't be that race to find the next supplement, vibrational tool or tuning forks, or the next healer, or next process. For some, your whole world's simply going to begin opening; and it will continue to open and to amplify.

Whoever said that you could only use two percent of your brain, or ten percent? Whoever said that you couldn't access all your abilities and open up to everything and to all possibilities? You were taught to be average. But who created an average to begin with? There really is no such thing. As a matter of fact, when you contemplate things you don't resonate with "average" whatsoever. Sometimes you feel completely more than average, very high above average. And then, oops, you realize you're not allowed to feel that way because if you feel more than average that's too egoic. And what if you are above average? Is more going to be asked of you? Are you going to have to be more responsible? While you're pondering these questions, you realize that no one you meet is really average. All are remarkable, uniqued beings.

You wonder what will happen now that you are beginning to honor yourself, starting to re-contemplate yourself. Many of you were taught not to do this, because of your faith or religion. And what is religion about? You do what you are "supposed to do," assuming that if you behave according to the rules, when you leave the body vehicle you'll be okay. You'll be welcomed in through the metaphoric pearly gates because you've earned the right. But what about enjoying heaven in a body on a planet? Now as you start to re-contemplate, you can start to tune into and feel your own presence, your own dimensional planes, and all the brilliant facets of who You are.

This is just one step, a step based in the vibratory levels of expansion, moving into a state in-between the in breath and the out breath. It is this space between in breath and out breath where you can feel yourself begin to re-emanate. You've let yourself come to the forefront to reactivate telomeres, reactivate the DNA. The fountain of youth is coming back to life in and through you. It's not about an exercise program or a diet, but about a complete reactivation. That reactivation is only the first part. Now you can welcome in the Creator essence that you are. You can welcome in your manifest levels, your Creator levels, your higher levels. You can welcome in the complete amplification and activation of the Christ consciousness within you, the amplification and activation of what I call your Crystallis state. You can welcome integrity with All That Is—not from a rule book of integrity, but from your natural state of honoring, embodiment and fluidity. You're opening yourself to your Universalis state because you are letting your Universalis levels take command. Your Universalis DNA, which is completely eternal and endless, can now become re-activated and amplified.

When you let yourself be clear and give your DNA permission to fully and completely re-activate, you'll begin to go through many amplifications. Some call this "downloading," when information is presented for you from your higher levels. I call it amplification, activation through your brain chemistries. As the master cells of your body vehicle are opening and rebuilding, you let everything outside of you be outside and completely separate from you. But how is this different from the separation between you and brother humanity? This separation means that the world is there for you to walk through, to have fun in. But you are no longer identified with or affected by belief systems, you are becoming completely immune to them instead. Now we're talking about your true Universalis DNA.

When your eyes aren't focused on what's beneath you, or even what's above you, you become wide open to everything. Now you can welcome in your big guns. "Show me," you say. "Show me what it is I am to know. Show me the gifts this day has to offer. Show me how I can best speak from complete clarity, neutrality, freedom, wide-openness, presence, essence, and eloquence." You are no longer requiring to be heard, no longer needing anything, because there's truly nothing that you need any longer. As you are opening and emanating all of You, which is beyond words, watch how complete clarity and purity emanate from you.

To metamorphosize is to let changes take place within you. And you are constantly metamorphosizing, constantly changing, evolving, and becoming You once again through the physical. You are changing constantly to further complement yourself, to complement your own personal journey, and the journeys of all those around you. It means recreating and letting the body be recreated, going beyond the identificational realms, stepping into the real You through the physicality. This is about the evolvement of the higher through the lower, as you are now coming into your true potential, and also your true nature. And please know that as this metamorphosis is taking place, You, your body and your world are all changing at once.

You're letting continual change come in and be presented for you. You're calling in your big guns, your higher levels, to completely complement you. The changes that are happening are about disengagement from the old magnetic ways, the old magnetic worlds, the old magnetic layers and levels. Now you can let yourself begin to open, and open, and open, to fully and completely embody your presence, your divinity.

What do you do when you have all of the answers presenting for You, from You, to You? Are there any major questions that need to be answered? Is there anything except letting you enjoy the brilliance, the heart, the love, the camaraderie of others? Now you're playing so much further with your Universalis DNA. And now your Universalis DNA can and will continue to amplify. You're beginning to question, and let the answers present. You're beginning to open to what's being presented. You're not holding yourself back. You're opening to the evolution of humanity. It's what's happening for you as you're ascending home. You're welcoming all of these abilities into activation and you're re-opening and moving into total communion with All That Is. You, as Creator Incarnate, from a complete, pristine, amplified Crystallis state, are embodying and opening to everything.

If you were to look at a Crystallis state, there are so many different facets involved. Have you noticed that they never end? What of the old theories of cause and effect, where one action would cause a certain reaction? Now, you are waking up and re-embodying your own divinity, your higher levels, Creator levels, and much, much more. All of the reactions based on the cause no longer apply and are not absolute any longer. This is because you have stepped into a new world and have superseded all of the density based in old magnetics, i.e., the karmic grid system. What you just stepped into is your eternal Beingness. As you step into your eternal Beingness let's celebrate and have more fun than ever. Because dear heart, you are in a body on a planet and you are home as Creator re-awakening and marrying with your physicality on all levels, expanding throughout this world. There is no end. And now we're talking about <u>complete</u> freedom.

MEDITATION ON REBUILDING THE DNA

You may wish to have someone read this meditation to you or record yourself reading it so you can follow along easily. Also, you can do these meditations with or without closing your eyes and over time you may experience that there is no need to close your eyes at all.

Let's go ahead and bring your consciousness right
into your pineal and pituitary glands
and as you're bringing yourself right into your pineal
and pituitary glands
and just simply hold the pressure there for a moment
and go ahead and call forth your master cells
and open up the master cells of the brain
and as you're opening the master cells of the brain
the beautiful pearl of essence has asked that it be
opened up
and let's call forth your DNA
the two double helix strands
and let's go all the way up the chain
let's ask that all of it begin to reactivate
to slide it up from the bottom

all the way to the top
all the way to the end caps, the telomeres
let's replace it with new telomeres
the beautiful little end caps that have been breaking
away, breaking away, and breaking away
and as fast as they become regenerated
revived
recreated
just let the pressure grow
going all the way down from your pineal and pituitary
glands
through your skull
through the back of your brain
down your central nervous system
down through your thoracic vertebrae
through your lumbar vertebrae
through your sacrum
through your sciatic
down your upper leg
down the back of your bottom legs
your lower legs
through the feet
all the way up through the front of the feet
through your shins
through your knees
to your patellar ligaments
all the way up through the front of your thighs
your upper front legs
right up through your gender principle
through your abdomen
your colon
your intestinal tract

through your anatomic nervous system
parasympathetic nervous system
all the way up through your heart
your sternum
through your throat
right up through your pineal and pituitary glands
again
into your DNA
the flaccid DNA becoming amplified again
and how's it beginning to feel
can you feel your particles moving around?
how's it feeling?
can you feel the buzzing going on?
that's the DNA

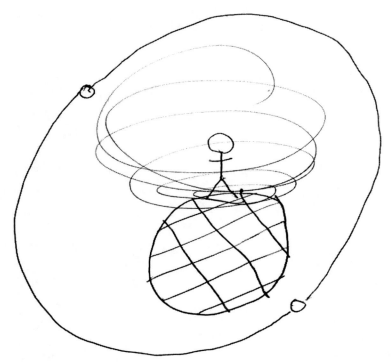

Your higher levels are what connect you to the Universe. When you are in touch with this higher self, you are in touch with all Consciousness. This is your ever-expanding Creator essence.

Chapter 5

PLAYING WITH HIGHER STATES OF CONSCIOUSNESS AND YOUR GUIDANCE REALMS

When things happen that can't be explained with science and accepted logic, brother humanity likes to call them miracles. A dear one with terminal cancer is suddenly cured. Another walks away from a terrible car accident without a scratch. A dear brother's car breaks down, and he gets a ride from the person who will offer him a new career. Or a voice in someone's head says, "Take this way home today," and she meets the love she has been waiting for all of her life. Then there are all of the "small" miracles that happen for you more every day: You seem to have these psychic abilities, picking up the phone before it rings, or answering a question before it's asked. You have a knowingness that keeps growing stronger.

Although humanity tends to call these events miraculous, I just call them natural. You see, your natural state allows for miracles, for complete clarity to take place. When you're in a state of clarity, you realize that you know things you've been taught you shouldn't—or couldn't—know. As you open up to your higher realms, miraculous events start to find you. You begin to understand that you have the ability to play with much higher states of consciousness than you ever thought possible. As the marriage of your higher and lower levels take place, you have the ability to play with these higher states of consciousness and your guidance realms to receive special knowledge and wisdom.

So what actually happens as the marriage of your higher and lower levels takes place? What does it mean to play with higher states of consciousness? First you open up to your higher levels, allowing them to steer and guide you. When you open up to your manifest levels, your creator levels, things that cannot take place from a simple belief system point of view start happening all the time. As you begin to be comfortable in the mystical realms, you learn to go direct, to let things present in your out-picturing world. You learn to access and follow your own guidance realms with greater ease. This means looking within, looking to You for the answers.

We've touched on the karmic grid system and the hold it had over all humanity for eons. That grid system was magnetized in the three lower chakras, keeping dear ones locked into a sex-power-greed dynamic through many life streams. As the grid system dissolves, humanity is opening to the three highest level chakras. These are the throat, the third-eye and the crown-level chakra vortexes, your higher levels, your guidance levels. As this occurs, the kingdoms begin to arise around you, and you become so much more aware. In turn, the awareness from these mystical realms is letting brilliant priceless changes happen within you, and you gain ever greater access to your higher realms. Your life becomes filled with the clarity that allows you to go direct.

So what do I mean when I talk about "going direct"? What is that, anyway? Going direct is going with the first answer that presents, going with the first dynamic that presents, walking through the first door that presents. It's a state of living beyond the mind level of comprehension and beyond the mind level of clarity. As I've said before, the mind is always striving to protect you. The mind does not want you to try something you've never tried before, or to seek an alternate path. But as you are stepping into You on every level of creation, you're going beyond what's ever been taught at the mind level. You're going beyond what's been imagined in ways that could never be comprehended or figured out by the mind level. This is because you're learning to live at the heart level.

Remember the example of the dear one who found her beloved just by taking a different way home? Why would she decide to drive in a new direction when she had literally been following the same direction for years? This is what I mean by going direct. It is following your own knowingness, your own clarity, your creativity. It's following everything that's opening up right before you. As you're listening to that voice, it's speaking right to your Creator consciousness. This is what is meant by "following your heart."

When you learn to let things present rather than try to <u>make</u> them happen, you are giving permission and the go-ahead for manifestations to come to you from your higher levels, your expanded states. They offer opportunities for you, ideals of creativity for you, ideals of creation for you so that you can begin creating changes in your outside world. And when you give the go-ahead to your higher levels to let things present, you are also giving the go-ahead to the angelic, archangelic and ascended host realms to begin assisting you overtime. Now, when we spoke of the Law of Attraction and the concept of manifesting, I explained that this way of looking at things ends up limiting you. When you play with your higher levels, when you give the go-ahead, you're not seeking a certain manifestation. Instead you're letting the manifestation find you, you're giving it permission to come into your life stream. So be it, and so it is. This is one and the same with "Let there be light," and there was light. It was not about "There <u>must</u> be light." It was about <u>letting</u> the light come into the world.

Love is presence as an unconditional state when you're letting yourself express. Love is the true Creator of All That Is, beyond intention, beyond energy, beyond consciousness. Oddly enough, in this state of communion, in this newly awakened state, brother humanity looks very different to you. For example, when you went to lunch the other day you were eating a hot dog on the street. And for the first time you truly noticed the children on the planet; you actually noticed the brilliance in their eyes. You may have always thought they were something to carry, or a job to do, and you had to take responsibility for their happiness, their growth; you had to think about teaching them. Maybe that's why you never had any children. Or maybe you had ten, and even though you were taught that you must love them, you could feel nothing except heavier with every day that went by. But then, the child that you saw at the hot dog stand had the most brilliant spark in her eyes; she reminded you of something. Could it be that what you saw was a reminder of the spark of divinity that a child is, that You are?

We've talked about the Law of Attraction and manifesting. But now you are playing with true manifestations, giving permission to your higher levels and going about your daily activities from complete availability. And you're beginning to express and to explore further all of your abilities. That's the true beauty of it—you're becoming You again. I am referring to the space between the thoughts, beyond the mind, without emotion, not out of the body but very much in it. In this space you're letting the mind turn off as you are feeling the emanation of You.

Remember the mind can't <u>feel</u>. Feeling is not emotion; feeling is beyond emotion. There is no resentment, guilt, repressed anger, frustration, or any other colorful emotions. There isn't a name. You can call this feeling love, but I choose not to, due to all of the definitions given to love. Even the term "unconditional love" has been given too many definitions. So let's call it "presence." It really has no specific definition. The mind will try to grab onto the words, but there's nothing for it to grab onto. Presence is the real You beyond the beliefs. Presence is You beyond the identifications, beyond limitations. Now from beyond the physical you step forward through the physical, feeling your essence, energy, presence, eloquence, and divinity.

I ask you, what would it be like if you were not trying to think happy thoughts, or think good thoughts, or trying to avoid bad thoughts? What would it be like to have no thoughts? Because when you are open to the day, when you have no thoughts, no preferences, you allow everything to come into your life stream. You say, "Let it present," and all possibilities are within reach. Taking a new way home is about letting things present. It is about going beyond the mind level.

For eons the soul level of consciousness had been running your underlying behavioral mannerisms beyond the conscious and subconscious. Residing in your lower chakras, the soul level was completely enmeshed in the karmic grid. The soul level attracted and brought forward different karmic journeys for you to wake up from and bring to resolution. Every life stream was very much based in a karmic dance. But that dance is one that has played out, that you have now outgrown and gone beyond. The soul has also been a record keeper of all of the victim/victimizer states you've lived through, the different formulas and alignments that have played out in your life streams. These records no longer have power over you. Because now you're going beyond the soul level of consciousness. You're going through the akashic record realms that have recorded every experience your soul has ever had from first separation to now. And you're calling those experiences complete and done. There is no longer anything to make up for—no karma to balance out—there is only life to be danced with. In effect, the ego is dissolving.

It may seem a bit alarming. This new way of being doesn't come with instructions. But that is because there really isn't a lot of difference between instructions and religion. Now life can be completely playful. "Show me what that truly means," you say. "I don't get it. What does it really mean to be open and expanding as Creator Incarnate? I've been taking responsibility since I was age two. And oddly enough, I still couldn't make anyone happy or gain their complete approval, no matter how hard I tried. Now you're telling me to just let go, let my ego die?"

You must let go. To break down the ego is to let the real You begin to arise. This is the timeless You that has always been. And You are arising to address the egoic state of consciousness. As you're letting the egoic structure dissolve and fade away, what you'll find is that it has many voices. It has the world, it has the mass consciousness, it has mom and dad. The ego has so many voices within it, but the one voice that is missing is yours. So when you dissolve the ego, you begin by questioning it, asking where it comes from. You ask, "Whose voice am I listening to?" You listen carefully, and you hear the familiar "I think, I should, I ought, I must." You hear judgment and fear.

But how many times have you heard another voice in your head, one that seems to be guiding you, comforting your mind? You are getting these brilliant ideals that seem to be taking you in a new direction. If you listen carefully, the voice is always calm and loving. This is the voice of your guidance realms connecting. Your guidance realms have always been around you, wanting to be accessed, wanting to be heard. This guidance is there to be enjoyed and explored. But how do you access your guidance realms? How do you remain in touch with the higher You? You simply step back from the world and ask, "Which way should I go? What is in my highest and best good?"

The first answer that comes to you is from your guidance realms. It will embody the ideals of creativity and clarity, showing you the pathway and guidance to let you succeed and flourish. The first step is to go with your guidance realms, to follow them, and see what's on the other side. As you're taking the information and going with it, moving with it, following it, you'll start to find that the guidance becomes stronger, becomes clearer.

A voice will present that says, "Read the paper today." You may never read the paper, but you go with what's presenting at the moment; you listen to that voice. And there will be an article that opens a door for you. Your guidance realms will also present what would be the most impactful about your journey to speed up the process and the unfoldment of You. I won't pretend—sometimes the unfoldment can be painful. And I won't ask you to try for the Enlightenment Olympics, to smile when you've just lost your house and someone's run over your dog. Yes, the world presents every type of experience. But what a brilliant unfoldment it is! You soon find yourself dancing with it, even in the difficult times, even in pain and sadness. Then something else presents that will bring you the greatest happiness—because <u>nothing</u> is static. My own journey in this body was filled with physical pain at first, but I could feel that my angel was waiting for me. Experiencing that pain helped me clear the decks and be done with that chapter.

Your guidance realms are giving you signposts and directions that assist so much further in complementing where you're going and how you're getting there, and taking the simplistic route to speed up the process. I encourage you to listen and run with what these higher levels tell you. Let's not think about what they say, let's follow it, because guidance will never lead you astray. Guidance is wisdom and clarity coming from You, to You, through You, opening up your world. What do I mean when I say that guidance comes from You, to You and through You? Remember that your internal guidance realms are a part of you, and that guidance speaks from your higher self. This part of you doesn't thrust itself forward the way the egoic structure does. Your guidance realms don't attempt to take control the way the mind level does. Instead your higher levels are patiently waiting for you to recognize them.

As we start to explore your ability to play in higher realms, let your mind go for a moment. Let's take your consciousness from your heart to the sun, and back to your heart. Now watch and notice how you become disengaged from all of the scenarios around you, as you're bringing yourself up through the body vehicle to higher states of consciousness. You're not thinking about relationships, or the school system, or work, or family, or food, or even world peace. You truly disengage from these different preoccupations that you've been acting out. Once you see the preoccupations for what they are, watch how these little particles of thought forms that have been floating around in your auric levels begin to dissolve.

Let's honor that the mind may still be afraid. The mind says, "I've got to hold on to this identity and these perceptional beliefs. I've got to stay on top of all situations; I've got to take care of all of this stuff around me. Because if I don't take care of all of the outside world beliefs and perceptions, the identities with jobs, with abundance levels, with looks, with position, it's all going to collapse and go away." Yet no matter how tight its grasp, the mind loses its control and is unable to hold onto the ways of the old paradigm. As this is occurring for you, remember to comfort the mind. Tell it that all is well. When you go beyond the old structures, the old paradigmal states, you allow yourself to experience true freedom.

We've spoken about giving the go-ahead, letting your day present rather than forcing anything. Pay attention to what happens when you go beyond all of the old beliefs, when you say to your guidance realms, "Show me. Show me that you're real, beyond belief, beyond my senses. I want to finally feel the true comfortability of being in a body on a planet. The comfortability of being myself, the camaraderie that I've heard so much about from all these groups, and books, and seminars. I really want to communicate and feel my own divinity."

Some who are further along their own journey may have a little more of a dialogue with their guidance realms. Those who are much further along their own journey may actually see the answer, as well as hearing it through conversations with their higher levels. In these cases the mind level receives pure clarity, and you will use the mind to transcribe and receive the clarity and purity. And the answers present to you, as you are beginning to receive a whole new type of communication with these realms. Even though everyone on the planet has these abilities, it is only now that humanity is truly beginning to ask and receive the answers, beginning to act on and explore them. How beautiful and how familiar it feels to communicate with your higher levels! It seems like home beyond the physical. And then you're bringing this presence here through the physical. Can this be real? Well, you're experiencing it. What do you think?

What if you begin to ask your guidance realms if they're real? Why not examine them a bit further? You are presented with all this data, all of these beautiful ideals that just flow to You, through You. And your guidance realms are saying softly, "Just give us a chance." Of course you know there's something going on there. But the mind has a hard time believing. "Doesn't this seem a little bit too good to be true?" the mind asks. "Shouldn't you have to work to hear these voices? Don't you need to focus, to <u>try</u>?"

And then you listen again to those whispers, those subtle thought forms that are presenting. "Just give us a chance," the voices whisper. "Dear heart," they say, "we love you so dearly, but we also know how uncomfortable it is to <u>be</u> you. We know that for all these years you've been forcing yourself to fit in. You've been told that if you don't fit in something cataclysmic is going to happen. You may have been deemed different from

everyone else and separate. You may be afraid of the
death of the ego, of the loss of power and control.
You may fear being ostracized, not being important,
not mattering. And we honor all of that. All we ask
is that you start to give us a chance to show you. You
don't have to make believe. We're here to show you
that we have you taken care of. We can't live for you,
but we want to assist you, because remember we are
here and have always been here to honor and assist
you as our family. Remember, You are waking up in
creation."

"So let's explore a little more," the voices continue.
"All of this may seem a little bit grandiose. But let us
do our part, dear heart. The only thing we're asking is
you let us show you that we're real, that we're here. Let
us do our part, with You and for You." As you start to
come to terms with this familiarity, you are beginning
to remember instances within this incarnation when
you felt those realms and trusted them. Do you recall
what you were going through until age twelve, in your
"formative" years? There was that nudge and nagging
that kept calling to you. And yet you were so afraid to
listen to that voice, to act on it, because everyone else
ignored their calling. Your parents, your family, even
your closest dear ones had forgotten about their guidance realms and were not listening.

The higher self, the idea that you had guidance
realms, was never talked about. And you had to ask
yourself, "Why am I different? Why am I odd? Is there
something wrong with me?" The funny part is, this
familiarity has been here to show you and to assist
you, to help you along your way. Are you now going

to start to follow your nudge, your calling, your guidance? Looking back you realize that when you have done this, when you have followed them, nothing has ever been chaotic or disruptive. And you know that you will never be let down.

Can you see how differently you feel? Wow! What a brilliant world that's opened up for you, one where nothing will ever be topsy-turvy any longer. You don't have to walk on a tight wire anymore. You don't have to follow a strict rule anymore. You certainly don't have to listen to the chaotic states that you've been taught to listen to, from all that was taught and experienced. When you begin to play and explore this resonance, these voices, these gentle nudges, have you noticed that odd things start to change within your physicality? Your hair may stand on end, your whole spine that you were taught could never rebuild itself suddenly feels like it's nine years old again.

After all these years of going through negative scenarios, how can changing be this easy? And yet it is. How could this have happened without all of the processing that you were taught? You were taught that it would take so many more years—even lifetimes—to get to a breaking point of neutrality, to be able to move forward. Now watch how all of the dear ones who have really intimidated your mind level because of their "enlightenment" status no longer have the power to intimidate you. And what freedom this brings! You are now free from having to eat a certain way, drink a certain way, dress a certain way, live a certain way. You are now free to be in your natural state. "Can it really be that simple?" the mind asks.

Remember that your guidance levels let you listen to the ones around you from your expanded states. Now that you're disengaged, you can let yourself become fully and completely open. You don't have to play out the same scenarios—the same conversations, the same arguments, the same ways of dealing with people. As you're letting yourself be fully and completely clear, this is where you're welcoming the facet of Creator you are. You welcome in the "I Am" presence, the higher levels, the manifest levels, the Creator levels, and all of these different attributes of You can start to take command. Imagine allowing these guidance realms—these gentle, loving voices—to take command of your soul, your life, your work, your mind, your body, your world. Now taking command of your finances, taking command of your opportunities, as you're becoming wide open again. Listening to your guidance realms means letting go of the control of the little you, i.e., the egoic levels that have been holding you back and running your life. When you allow your higher levels to take command, you are no longer a slave to circumstances.

As the higher You, you're not going to carry any psychic baggage. And you can begin to watch the day as it presents, and have a blast. You are now free from getting hijacked into one conflict or another. It starts with the simple things. You can really enjoy driving because you aren't wanting to run the dear brothers around you off the road. You can stand in line without getting impatient. You don't get upset when things change at the last minute. You, as Creator, are letting yourself have everything and beyond. You have the enjoyment of optimum physical health and well-being, the enjoyment of abundance throughout your life; and there are so many different sorts of opportunities presenting to fully and completely be enjoyed. You are really connecting, feeling such love emanating from your heart center. And when things are complicated or difficult, when a dear one leaves the planet, for example, you know that this is also part of creation. Your higher levels, your guidance levels are there to comfort you.

As you hand your life over to your Creator essence, all is available. Ask your guidance levels to take over the finances, and then watch what happens as the first door presents. Okay, there's an opportunity behind Door #1. "It doesn't look very abundant," cautions the mind. But your guidance says, "It presented, so let's go through it." And what is behind Door #1 turns into the opportunity of a lifetime. Wow! Here come all of these different connected states. Dear brothers are wanting to come into your life stream to complement you, to fully and completely offer the great beauty of a camaraderie, a dance together. You are now in a state of being free from the attachment to an outcome. So you say, "Thanks for coming in," and you let yourself begin to enjoy the dance. And you notice that as you're enjoying the dance, everything somehow takes care of itself, much more easily than the little mind could have comprehended.

You're not believing anything, you're not hoping, you're not trying to manifest. You're just letting yourself have a blast. You're just enjoying all of the brilliant, beautiful attributes around you. And you're not <u>trying</u> to enjoy yourself, or have a good life. It's happening naturally. You're letting the world be what it is;

you're not being hijacked into the old patterns. You're not preoccupied by the same old questions: "Will I succeed? Will I find a relationship? Will I do what I want to do in this life?" Instead, you're just fully and completely enjoying the unfoldment. Not because you're trying, but because you're allowing. What you're also doing is letting all sorts of different brilliant opportunities come into your life stream to be fully enjoyed, to be fully embodied, to be fully embraced, to be fully expressed.

Once again things aren't happening because you've decided, "I'm trying to express." Instead you're letting yourself be in a fluid natural state, where You as Creator are free to let all of creation take care of itself. You're simply sitting and expanding into the overview and being disengaged, letting everything continue to run its own course, and getting to change with ease. You can be completely disengaged because you already know full well as Creator Incarnate that there's no real harm that could come your way. There's no lack coming your way, no real struggle. You as Creator have commanded it so. What you're going to do is simply be yourself, let your own presence be known and expressed by stepping into your true divinity, your true power. You find yourself walking your own walk, and having a blast with who you are, not who the mind level thinks you are or should be.

And what happens to the world outside you? All of the brilliant dear brothers around you can now also begin to be present to be fully and completely embraced and enjoyed. You are being and emanating the Creator brilliance that you are, not because you're hoping to be Creator, but because you're simply <u>being</u> Creator. You have been and are being given every confirmation so that you no longer have to attempt to wake up and remember. You have awakened.

Everything else that you have been asking for can now fall right into alignment, right into place. But please don't think about a timeline. You aren't going to say, "I will have the perfect job by this date," and then sit and concentrate on that perfect job. Everything can now be in a fluid state, which is your natural state without all of the emotional ups and downs. Now the fact that you are in a fluid state is why you're still not engaged. You're so busy having a great time, you're so busy enjoying having a physicality. You begin to revel in the corpuscles of touch, the eyesight, all the senses. You're just letting yourself be wide open to let everything else take its own course. You are not demanding of the Universe, not demanding that perfect job. You are confident that the job will come, and you do what is necessary to get it, without effort, without force.

You see, you are no longer engaged in the world. You are no longer attached to one certain outcome, putting all this hope and energy into it. You are completely wide open to everything. Because when you were in that engaged state where you were becoming so fixated on one certain dynamic, one certain outcome, you cut yourself off from everything but that one certain outcome. So, as you have no intent focus on a specific job, for example, you are allowing yourself to be open to every job. Many may say, "Well, you need to focus to be able to live in a body on a planet or to manifest." And I say, "Absolutely not." The lack of intense focus <u>truly</u> lets you be in a body on a planet. You can let the body vehicle be the body vehicle, let it do its part by being in optimum health and well-being, constantly regenerating itself. You can let the mind be the mind and allow it to be a processor of information. And you can rely on your higher levels to guide you.

So what about being able to play in a work environment? What about the dear brother who has no special type of education, no credentials, no experience, yet continues to move up the corporate ladder? How can that be? It's because that brother's success is not about the education, the credentials, or the experience. Instead it's about letting one's own presence be in charge. That brother is not attempting to go up a ladder, or down a ladder, or off a ladder. He is simply dancing with the experience.

It's the same with you. You're not trying, you're not engaged. You're just showing up and going with everything that's happening around you. You're going with what's presenting, not getting hooked in or hijacked, or becoming identified with a situation. You simply begin to allow yourself to ask, "How best can I have a blast today? What is the journey at hand? Okay, great!" And then you say, "Let's play with it. Let's build it. Let's re-build it. Let's move it forward." Watch how your fluidity, your divinity, your clarity increase. New opportunities will present for you, such as promotions and more abundance, and they will present without your intense focus.

Science gives us great examples of how intense focus can actually be so limiting. What do scientists do when they narrow down to one type of research, or look for one specific equation? They become totally locked in. The answer is right there before them, if only they would let themselves see it. If they would let themselves be open, the equations and formulas would come with great ease. And this is what you're doing, simply letting yourself continue to open, and to open, and to open, losing the narrow focus that has kept you locked in. And this is where we are playing with creation. You're letting creation begin and continue to present for you, just as you asked, just as you gave permission as the facet of Creator that you are.

With the help of your guidance realms, you'll have a lot of humor and clarity as well as still being in constant movement and wide openness. You're living in a fruitionary state, a state of creating, a fluid state that has no trying involved. Do you see? Because it's already You. Now you're beginning to welcome in your higher self. You are going beyond the mind, beyond the physical, yet <u>through</u> the physical levels and the mind levels that are your friends. Let's not give our power away and get caught up in all these big giant myths of the ego. The mind is your friend now, it's under control. And the ego no longer has the power to run your life or how you feel. Now you are re-arising into who you really are, rather than the old karmic paradigm of who you were supposed to be or should be.

You and all of brother humanity are now displaying the great brilliance and beauty you've always had that's coming back to the forefront. That's why so many dear brothers are having mystical experiences, so many are having shamanic experiences. Dear ones are participating in tribal ceremonial memories and experiences, from the sweat lodges, to the different groups chanting. Now you are free to enjoy these mystical experiences.

Here's a radical thought: You're already healed, so let's be done with the quest for perfection! You can start enjoying your health and vitality to its fullest on every level. You can be truly blessed by the Universe that is yours, that is You. Your part is to let things happen, and to walk through your day being available and open, welcoming in your guidance levels to show you the way. Give yourself the go-ahead to honor the work now being done, even if it feels like play. "Thanks," you say. "I'm going to sit back and enjoy the unfoldment of opportunities coming in. I'm giving them permission to unfold." There are times you will be presented with an idea out of "nowhere" that really comes from your guidance realms. So please follow that guidance, and once you've done your part, let the rest of the details take care of themselves as your higher levels step in. Then watch what takes place for you in the outpicturing world.

MEDITATION ON PLAYING WITH HIGHER STATES OF CONSCIOUSNESS

You may wish to have someone read this meditation to you or record yourself reading it so you can follow along easily. Also, you can do these meditations with or without closing your eyes and over time you may experience that there is no need to close your eyes at all.

Let's bring your consciousness right back through
your heart
turning off the rest of the world
and from there, let's bring your consciousness up
through your throat
your pineal and pituitary glands
your crown chakra level vortex
opening up your crown chakra level vortex
letting it continue, and continue and continue to
open
and to amplify
to twenty feet above you
opening up approximately 18 feet wide
continuing to let it arise, and arise, and arise
and to open

bringing your consciousness through the atmospheric realms
welcoming in your higher levels
to begin to speak to you, steer you, and journey you
and as you are bringing your consciousness to the sun
let's look back down upon the planetary matrix
through the eyes of creator, and the eyes of Horace
welcoming in a whole different state of clarities
a whole different state of realities
through the atmospheric realms
through the crown chakra level vortex
welcoming in a brilliant stream of gold
a brilliant stream of light
to run right through you
for you, from you
and all of the accessibilities that you have available
around you
and look upon all those around you
and what they're going through where they're at
and welcome them, your brilliant realms of gold
as you're in this state
and as you're at this state
let's welcome in your big guns to take command™
to speak through you, steer you, and journey you
can you feel how high your consciousness is right now
how clear everything is
let's bring your consciousness back to your pineal and
pituitary glands
and open your eyes
and how clear does everything look

now that you've broken energy
you've disengaged
you've opened up again
to get to play overtime
and how is your body feeling
and how clear does it feel
this is playing with your higher states of consciousness
and also creates revitalization

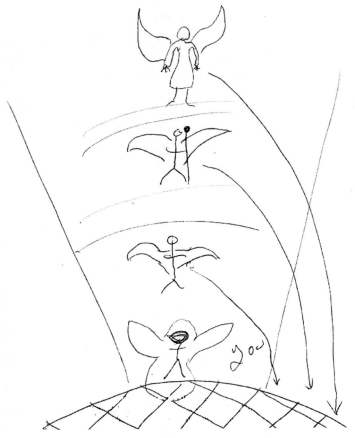

You are unified with your higher and lower selves. Your angelic, archangelic and ascended host realms are pictured above You. These other realms constantly are communicating with You.

Chapter 6

COMMUNICATING WITH ANGELIC AND ARCHANGELIC PRESENCES AND ASCENDED HOST REALMS

Now we're going to take things further in this chapter. Because you haven't been let down, you can free yourself to be open, continuing to grow. The dear ones coming into your life are just absolutely amazing, and there are parts that you've been seeing within them that you're seeing within yourself. You find yourself expanding, growing, enjoying your life so much more. You really enjoy being in a body on a planet. This is life without all the dramas and emotional roller coasters. At this time you may find that you are having these odd, yet somehow familiar dreams about places, people, situations. These dreams are showing you more and assisting you to remember and open further. You're really beginning to step things up, so now let's step things up even more. In addition to communicating with your internal guidance realms, you have the ability to speak with angelic and archangelic presences, and ascended host realms. This chapter is about consciously enjoying the assistance and love of these guides.

Religions will tell you that only a special few can communicate with these sacred beings, and only in very special circumstances. But I can tell you that outside deities from the angelic, archangelic, and ascended host realms are here to further and fully complement you on your life's journey. Your higher realms are always communicating with them. They are walking with you side by side. As you continue to change, these external guidance levels begin to open up for you, letting their presences be known to You, and through You. Are you now going to give these dear ones an opportunity to speak? This is the availability you have been asking for. You are meant to be in a communicative state with them as they offer you support and clarity. And because you're right there dancing with them, they will let their presence be that much further known and accessed.

I refer to the angelic, archangelic and ascended host realms as "external guidance" because they are somewhat different from your internal guidance realms. You see, the internal guidance realms are really a part of You. They are the voices of your higher levels. Your external guidance realms—the angelic, archangelic, and ascended host realms—are your extended family. In effect, you call upon your angelic realms to be a part of your entourage, to assist your higher levels, just as you might call on your family and dearest friends, to assist you.

As you're welcoming in the angelic realms to be a part of your life stream, they're beginning to speed things up for you. How do they speed things up? They help you to recognize certain truths when you hear them. They help you to love more, to open your heart level. If your higher realms assist by giving you direction, your angelic realms assist by giving you a feeling of safety, of camaraderie beyond the physical. Your guidance realms are the ones who guide you through pathways as they are laid right before you. And your angelic/archangelic realms are standing by to assist you to walk through the world in your fullest of potential. They are the ones who assist in carrying you through.

In the last chapter, we spoke of the nudges you get from the internal guidance of your higher levels. So you can think of these external guidance realms as protectors, as advisors, even as cheerleaders. They encourage and support you. For example, you can call upon the archangelic realms to present doorways, to watch over the home, the kids. You can ask these dear brothers to watch over your property. They exist to help you find solutions to things that puzzle you. Your higher realms are always communicating with your angelic realms. As you continue to expand and open, you are going to be more conscious of playing with these external guidance realms throughout your day-to-day activities.

The angelic, the archangelic, and the ascended hosts all have different parts to play. For example, Archangel Michael can walk you right through the core of a battlefield. You become untouchable as he watches over all the outside attributes, clearing the way. As the way is being cleared, your guidance realms are just walking you through. The angelic realms are the subtle soft tones that you feel within your own Beingness; they speak of your own elegance and exquisiteness. They are there to communicate, to share data and information, as they walk with you side by side.

The ascended host realms are dear brothers who once embodied through the physical, such as the Buddha, Krishna, Sathya Sai Baba, Francis of Assisi, Mahatma Gandhi, Yeshua ben Joseph (Jesus), Mary Magdalene, and the Virgin Mother. All of these are dear brothers who woke up through the physical and superseded it. They woke up to their innate abilities; they made a full transition and they began a whole new journey. These dear ones achieved a marriage of the higher and the lower through the physicality. And although they will not be coming back through the physical world, they are now even more available beyond the physical to let their presence be known, to offer you eons of playtime and assistance as teachers and guides. These ascended masters have been working overtime to assist brother humanity to wake up to all worlds. As the veils fall away, as you wake up more each day to the true You, the guidance these dear brothers is offering grows moment by moment.

In certain situations I'll send forward the angelic realms to clear pathways so that I and the ones with me show up equal to whatever dynamic presents. Imagine I'm on my way to the Bellagio Hotel on New Year's Eve. And there are suddenly all kinds of fireworks going off all around Las Vegas and the Strip, thousands of people, lots of chaos. I say, "All right archangelic realms, take command!" From there I'm going to be walking with my guidance realms and angelic realms right down the road to the Bellagio, completely untouchable. There are no crazy drivers, no traffic jams; there is no human drama. My big guns—my higher levels and my angelic entourage—come forth to play with me, separating me from the dramas, taking me all the way to my destination.

You and your guidance realms are now becoming friends, working together in a camaraderie with your mind and body. Have you noticed that you are now being presented with more clarity and manifestations, more wisdom? Please welcome these in. Have you also noticed that these external guidance realms tell you the impossible is entirely possible? Please give them the go-ahead. Because you keep getting these thoughts which seem a little bit unbelievable. And what about your talks with them? You've been hearing and learning about angels for some time now, and you think there is a certain way to speak to them. You have read about these angelic presences at the closest neighborhood metaphysical bookstores, and those books you've read tell you that only dear brothers with special gifts can be in touch with angels.

And so you've been taught that you're not the type to speak to angels or ascended hosts. But now you've been hearing these voices inside, voices of purity and love beyond what you have read in your biblical indoctrinations. So, you wonder, if you continue to welcome the actual angelic presences in, do you still need to give your power away to the tarot readers, or the angel card readers, or to the "mystics"? It may be the priests, the rabbis, the gurus or the sages who you've been

taught to think you should listen to, who are suppos-
edly so much further along on their journeys. But do
you really need to go to India so that you can come
to terms with your own being? What do you need to
learn? The answer is, you need learn nothing to step
into your divinity. And this is why you are beginning
to hear these higher levels now. And they are so honored that you are listening to them. They are honored
to begin sharing with you, as you are giving them the
permission to let their presence be known.

You are reading right here that you need to do
nothing except follow and listen to this calling, and see
this clarity about yourself that has been there for years,
that has really always been there. You're beginning to
remember different events that you have experienced
where these presences must have been watching over
you, these experiences that you've kind of sloughed
off or rationalized with your mind. There was the time
you heard your father's voice and later found out he
had already left the physical. There was the time you
appealed to the angels to help you with patience,
and you sailed through a difficult task. There was the
time you asked one of the ascended hosts, "What is
the right thing to do?" and immediately heard the
answer. Now you're beginning to remember the voices
you were hearing at the time. You can also remember
when those voices were suppressed and denied. Now
you can begin to let them come to the forefront. Now
you don't need to feel alone any longer, because they
have never left you and never will.

You've been afraid to speak with them because it all
seems so simplistic and fluffy. Could living be total and

complete simplicity, so simple that it's been missed for eons? How could that be? "I want to know the truth," you say. "What would happen if I let these dear ones come in further?" And then your mind chimes in: "Well, maybe I'm making it up. Show me again. I want to know that this is real." In a way your mind wants nothing more than to prove these beings don't exist. But can you feel your body warming up? Simply give yourself the go-ahead to let these dear ones speak to you, and watch what takes place.

So let's start playing with your external guidance realms. Let's start by welcoming forward the first dear ones who come to mind. From the expanded realms, let's start to welcome in their presence, whether it be in the palm of your hand, whether it be as an aura around you—whatever feels appropriate. Because what we're playing with is about welcoming You forward and also the dear brothers that have been around You. And as you start to do that, ask yourself: "What is it that I would like to know? What is it that resonates with me? I want to know what I want. I want to know what would open my heart to expand further."

Now let's start to welcome in these presences further by saying, "I want the confirmation that you're real." As you simply welcome forward their presences here, can you feel the three beings around you? In the front, and on the right, and on the left side of you—can you feel their essence? Let's ask for further confirmation. Let's welcome them to present different fragrances. And then what's the first fragrance that comes to mind? Can you actually smell that fragrance? Can you feel these beings, beyond just sensing, beyond intuition? Sensation and intuition are brilliant tools, yet this is a presence that you're welcoming forward. It is going beyond the mind, beyond the emotional realms, beyond the physical realm. The beautiful arms, the wings around you—can you start to feel them embracing and holding you with love and honor? For as much as you may honor them, your recognition is such a gift to them. They are honored that you recognize and welcome them into your presence, giving them permission to be an intricate part of your life stream.

We are speaking of trusting your higher levels, of dancing with your internal guidance and your external guidance. It is a state without blockages or conflict. This eternal guidance is a mindless state of hearing the clarity, the wisdom, the brilliance of You, from You. These guidance realms begin to show you a whole other pathway, and to walk you through the pathway of the heart, of love, of exquisiteness, prosperity, enjoyment. This guidance allows you to have everything beyond what the mind could have fathomed or comprehended. It's letting you step into a state that has always been You. It is your eternal nature, a timeless state of living beyond the clock. It's based in a place between worlds.

The angelic, archangelic and ascended host realms surround you and exist for the highest and best good of all. These presences are there to further complement your journey, to open you up and support you, to communicate with you and guide you. The angelic realms are about assisting you to a whole new realm and resonance of creation. They are there to assist you

in remembering your divinity. It is total and divine
support they want to offer, support to allow you to live
the life of your dreams—to live beyond the life of your
dreams. These presences are witnessing your new life
as Creator Incarnate, looking on with total love, passion, and compassion. They watch you amplifying and
running your course, and their only wish is to assist,
to walk you through the doorways and opportunities.
They are waiting for you to give them the go-ahead
to assist you in stepping into your God-given rights.
They are here to assure you that the true courage of
the whole Universe is not to be like another, but to be
yourself.

Your angelic/archangelic realms work with you
during your day hours and sleep hours, always calling,
always communicating, wanting to be acknowledged
by you. They are there to further assist your own pathway home, to assist you with your planetary Beingness
as you are remembering who you are. They assist you
in the embodiment of all your brilliant attributes and
innate abilities. These dear brothers love working with
your higher realms to create pathways and opportunities for you. And their great wisdom, their great abilities
within their own Beingness are assisting and activating
abilities within you. As you begin to hear these dear
brothers, you'll receive clarity. You'll become much
more open, much more diligent and courageous in
your journey to let the world be the world.

So you ask: "Guides, angelic presences, what do
you really have to share? Will you show me what you're
really about? Are you the ones that everyone keeps giving their power to, the ones who will bless me only

if I behave myself? Because I really don't know what 'behaving' means anymore as I'm reading this book." And do you feel it? Is your whole body beginning to experience such amazing tingling and energy shifts? Are the hairs standing up on your whole body; are there different sensations that you're feeling within the room? Now can you hear the tones, hear their laughter, sense their playfulness?

You wonder what this is really about. It's like that feeling many of you have at Christmas time, when so many surprises present, and there is the giving from your heart, when the love that You are is so present. There are those beautiful stories that really touch your heart, when there's so much of that tingling and familiarity within the stories. When you have these experiences, these are your higher levels and angelic presences at work, helping you to remember who you are and what this journey has truly been about.

For some of you there are all of these sense impressions, aromatics and beautiful memories coming to the surface. Well what are these memories about? Remember, based on your accepted metaphysical perceptional beliefs, you're not allowed to live in the past, and you can't live in the future—you can only live in the present. But what if all of these memories are presenting? Perhaps they have something to tell you. So you remember how much fun you had years ago on a simple fishing trip, at a simple picnic. You remember the wonderful time you had with the dear brothers around you, and you think to yourself, "I remember the experience with the bass fishing dear brothers all those years ago. It was the first time I felt loved, or embraced, or cared about."

Oddly enough, it was the dear ones you were with, but it was also so much more. That was the one time when you felt everything was really okay. You wonder what are these memories, what are they about? And now everything makes sense. You remember when you felt so all alone. Nothing really changed for you after that day, but you felt comforted; you suddenly felt safer being in a body on a planet. You actually felt loved. Remembering the feelings that came over you with this great love and great passion, you ask, "Was it my higher levels? Was it my angelic presences, my guides? Was it the stepping out of worlds? Or was it all of these things, offered to me so that I could feel and be open and embody the divinity and love that I am?"

Isn't it kind of odd that these memories are presenting? What has this been about? What was that presence when you really needed someone or something, when you felt so alone in the world, so separate from everyone and everything in the world, and nothing made sense? Do you remember lying in your bed and feeling others in the room? This was actually your angelic presences who were showing you that everything was okay, and was going to be okay. These presences told you that you have always been loved, and would always be loved no matter what. And were all of those different things that you kept hearing in your mind level? It was much more than your mind level. You were really hearing and feeling these angelic levels as you stepped out of time and began to embody and experience your true nature of divinity and so much more from beyond the mind.

The mind asks, "If I gave myself the go-ahead to begin to remember, and to play with the angelic realms, how could I even function in the world?" But are you now starting to come to terms with the fact that there is really so much more available for you than you thought? Whether you've been struggling with the perceptional importance of the bills, whether it be all of the societal rules in your marriage, whether it be the children and what you're supposed to teach them, whether it be the parents and the behavioral mannerisms they taught you, or whatever it may be. You kept hearing the subtle voices saying, "All is well. Everything is really okay. Remember who you are. Just walk through the day and enjoy the beauty of what is truly being presented."

You wonder, "Is that why in the midst of everything that was happening I noticed a certain beautiful fragrance of jasmine that continued to arise for me for days?" Can you remember what happened while you were walking through a garden, or Central Park, or anywhere and everywhere in this beautiful Eden we call the world? Did you notice everything that began to arrive for you? Could this be about being given and being presented with confirmations? Oh yes, dear heart. Your angelic presences—the ones who love you so deeply and dearly—were reminding you. Are you starting to get it? Are you starting to understand their love? Beyond getting it, are you beginning to see, remember, and embrace them? As you begin to question what is, what has been, and who you truly are, do you see how you're beginning to integrate this knowledge?

So let's ask your higher levels, your external guidance realms, your whole entourage: "Can I now begin to feel more love and to be more loved than ever? What is it that you have to show me today? What is it that you have to share with me?" It's time to remember the blessedness that You are, to remember that You are not just here to experience anymore. You've heard so much about how everything's an experience. You've heard that it's up to you to accept or not accept the experience. But that has so much to do with your mind level. As I've said before, your mind level never likes to be incorrect. It's always trying to be upright and justified, asking, "Am I doing the right thing? Did I do the right thing? Will I do the right thing?"

Can you see how your mind is always trying to run the show? You were taught that you had to take responsibility for your mind, taught that you were the mind. Now you know that the mind is just a small part of you. When you started thinking about changing your life, you were taught that you had to retrain the mind, to re-guide it. So now, as you call in your higher levels and external guidance realms to take command of your mind, are you giving away your power to an outside deity? Absolutely not! Rather you're letting yourself be loved, lightening the load and letting yourself be honored and at peace—open for so much more to be enjoyed. It may seem a little bit odd, but can you feel the familiarity and lightness? You know, it is the opposite of work to let your guides carry the work for you. It's pretty easy, a simple road to walk down. You'll no longer have to take responsibility for the density.

Now, rather than simply relying on the mind, you can allow your higher levels, the angelic presences and guidance realms in your life stream to carry the load for you. Haven't you started to notice those around you offering their divine assistance? It is a total and complete expanded dance they offer. Can you hear these realms like an echo of the Universe around you, within you? It is You. This has been You—the real You—all along. But are you sure you're ready for this one, for not engaging in all of the dramas? Seriously, why not give it a try?

I've seen this happen with so many dear ones. It could be that you just got a promotion, and all you did was to simply walk through your daily activities as you normally would, but with much more freedom and lightness. As a matter of fact, even though you aren't especially involved, you can't help but enjoy yourself more than ever. You find that you really don't have to earn the corporate Nobel Prize to move up positions. Your guidance realms, angelic and archangelic realms are there to show you, letting their presence be further known. Of course, you are still functioning in a body on a planet, so you may be afraid of others giving you odd looks for being different. But have you noticed? Other dear ones actually want to be around you more than ever. The ones you've been working with have suddenly started opening up to you. You've begun to know what they're really about.

Have you noticed how you've had tunnel vision, so focused on certain issues, about how you should, ought, <u>must</u> do the right thing? What about the belief that good guys always finish last, or good girls are always being taken advantage of? Are you starting to see that none of these beliefs are quite accurate? It was only what you were taught to believe so that you could fit in with all of the typical scenarios. These thoughts were passed on to you via others' perceptions about what it takes to get along in this world. Now with the aid of your guidance realms, you are seeing this world in a new light.

Haven't you noticed that these dear ones that you've only dreamed of want to be around you, can't wait to be around you, and would love to be able to communicate further? Now you can let your presence be known to them as well. You don't have to hide from them any longer. Of course, you are still living in a body on a planet. And you've met some dear brothers who seem to be way out there in some other planetary galaxy. When they spoke of communicating with angelic beings or presences, you may have thought they were crazy. And you may not want to experience that sort of life in a body because it seems to be very ungrounded, going to extremes rather than being yourself. There's a fine line here somewhere. So you ask all your guidance realms to show you that all is well. As you're beginning to feel safe you find you can listen further, open more. You will find that you don't have to behave a certain way or try to be something that you're not.

You've probably heard that we are all One, and all this kind of colorful stuff. And you may have tried to play with that belief, but it became so heavy. You've wondered, "If I'm you, you're me, and we're all each other, does that mean that everyone's unhappy? If so many dear brothers are unhappy, could that mean that we're all really unhappy in a deep, deep, dark place within?" You may have contemplated looking to the psychiatric realms for the answer. But you don't feel that way anymore. "We are all brilliance," says that quiet voice within. "Some are unhappy because they are trying so hard to get their own attention." Your new sense of knowing may scare you a little bit. But then you see a life that you've touched, another dear one who's given herself permission not to fall into the mass consciousness. You look around and see that so many others are just wanting to be themselves too. All around, you recognize dear brothers who are not wanting to fall asleep or get lost in the mind/ego. That unhappiness you have witnessed is simply about others wanting to maintain their clarity, wanting to wake up and stay awake without buying in to this world's taught perceptions.

So great job! You're beginning to see and experience that brilliant love of Creator Incarnate beyond the physical and through the physical in another. That's what freedom is really about. I still chuckle a little bit and scratch my head with this, because it really didn't take any work, did it? All of these years you've been working on yourself to get to that point, but once you quit working it actually happened. So now, wouldn't you love more confirmation? Wouldn't you love to feel your angelic realms more than ever? Can you hear them? Could you actually be speaking to the angel Gabriel? This choir of angelic voices doesn't sound like all the books say it should. You hear ring-ing tones and laughter going on in your body vehicle, your consciousness.

So you ask them: "Do you mean you guys have been here the whole time? Why didn't I discover this sooner? Because it would have been a whole different journey through this life. Have you always been here? Is that what those dreams were about? The life you showed me in my dream state just seemed too good to be true." Then the voice of your mind level comes back: "What in heaven's name is an ascended host? Because now you're really getting out there!" At one time, you would have listened to the mind and felt ashamed to be "out there." But you find that it's getting easier and easier to bypass the mind level's control.

You address the ascended hosts once again: "Do you mean you're really here to assist me? Do you mean you actually had a body and transcended it?" And your guidance realms reveal that the ascended hosts came here as a gift for humanity and a wake-up call. These dear brothers achieved what you would like to do. They brought light into the world. Now that you have played with the polarized state of light and dark, you can go beyond it into neutrality, light, love, divinity and the angelic realms. That means freedom. The ascended hosts woke up to who they were which is what you are doing now. Now they're here to help guide you. Why not ask for their assistance? "Guys, how did you do it? I've read about you in all of the perceptional history books that are called 'holy.' You received the assis-tance and the nudging too. So as I follow my heart and what I feel from this nudging, the message is that I can also do what you have done, and more. That certainly sounds amazing. Please, show me more."

You begin to see strange and wonderful events unfolding. For example, in the last three days you've gone to the coffee house, to restaurants, gone to all kinds of places. And no matter where you've gone, there have been many dramas taking place. It's like this morning at the coffee house, where the dear brothers were arguing among themselves and so angry. So you sat in the booth to have your coffee, and oddly enough, everyone lightened up. They actually began to open up and have fun together. In the midst of the dramas, when it looked at one point as though the authorities would need to be called upon, the change took place. "How is that possible ascended host realms?" you ask. "How can I be making a difference in the world just by being in that coffee house?" But you know that you <u>are</u> making a difference. "So I didn't attract that anger, did I? I dissolved it. And I didn't say a word. They felt my presence and my own divinity, just by my sitting in the booth."

You've been hearing about this energy dynamic. So are you now a conduit? And you wonder, "Is that why in the story books when you went into the many towns dear brothers, your presence created change? Is that why things opened up all around you? I thought that was just because you were the 'blessed' and 'holy' ones as the books say. You were emanating divinity. But am I also emanating this same divinity? Wow! Okay, now I really want to explore myself further because now these Law of Attraction principles that I have been playing with are kind of null and void—because I have

COMMUNICATING WITH ANGELIC AND ARCHANGELIC

outgrown them. Oh, yes, I do honor that I was playing with Michael when I played with those principles.
It was another expanded step along the way. So the
universal law principles do apply for those who are at
that point along their waking up process, but I want to
play further."

Your clarity grows further: "Okay, ascended hosts,
you want me to go to a bowling alley to be a conduit?
You want me to go to a casino? What I've been taught
by all of these different enlightenment groups is that
if you are in dense states, areas of 'darkness,' you will
become affected by dense energies. They teach that I
have to protect my energy, my light Beingness, my consciousness. So many groups and books teach us not
to go to these places. They say that 'like attracts like.'
But could light really be so fragile? If I show up at the
bowling alley, am I going to become someone different? Will I be affected by the darkness? Or can I assist
in opening them, in opening these people and places?
That seems like a pretty big load to carry. Is this how
you affected the whole world? Okay, I'll give it a shot.
I'm glad to know you'll be by my side because I've had
all these different callings, these nudges. I have been
feeling more like myself than I've ever felt. But now,
it's starting to become a reality beyond realities. Show
me more!"

Two linear days from the time you experienced the
bowling alley, and you're still kind of surprised by that
journey. Once again, there was chaos going on around
you, and it actually changed to be a very vibrant and
enjoyable place. A new thought pattern emerges for
you: "I don't really know about the bowling thing

because it doesn't really call to me a whole lot, but watching the dear ones around me was amazing. It was so odd because when I first arrived there were all these facial expressions, scowling and hostility. But then, the expressions would take a different shape; and people began to lighten up. Yes, I suppose Yeshua (Jesus) that I can start to honor the brilliance that I am, but I need a little bit more confirmation on it. You know, I'm still finding it tough to accept—because if I accept my birthright then I make such a beautiful life changing difference. Is that ego? I've thought that if I started to enjoy myself, if I started to see the love that I am, started accepting the love that I am, that I would create an inflated ego. I was always taught that to feel good about myself means I am ruled by my ego."

"So is that not quite accurate? Remember, I read many indoctrinations on so many subjects." So you ask yourself, "What are these indoctrinations really about? Are they of love? I wish only the best for all dear brothers. But love has no ego, and ego has no love. What is the basis for why these perceptions are revealing themselves? I'm glad you bring up these possibilities, Yeshua, because I never ever contemplated them. You're right. I'm not showing up to be noticed. I'm showing up to see what presents. That is a whole different realm of consciousness. There's so much more of the truth to that feeling; I know it is true because I can feel it within every particle and cell of my being. I know it, I can feel it. And I'm starting to feel a little bit better about myself and the way I am presenting."

"But let me ask one more time—if I feel good about myself is that the ego? No? So if I am simply being the

COMMUNICATING WITH ANGELIC AND ARCHANGELIC

expression of myself in my own uniquedness, is that the real me? I used to have a little bit of a conflict with that. What does my uniquedness mean? I'm supposed to like certain likings because I was taught to. What happens if I don't have the same likings that others partake in—for example, living off drama and playing in all of the energy games? I'm interested in other things. I've heard about all of these different abilities such as tele-transporting, etc. Do you mean I've already been using my special abilities from an unconscious state?"

You address the angelic choir. "Archangel Michael, you know I've heard about those battles from the heavens to the earth and all this kind of stuff. And now you tell me these stories weren't accurate. I've always been taught that the 'authorities' know so much more than I do. Please show me the whole truth." And now you realize that the visions about the battle between the light and dark were all metaphorical. In truth, it's the battle between your higher and lower levels, between your guidance realms and your egoic structure with all its beliefs and emotions.

You wonder about all these belief systems and judgments. If every belief you create means you're judging, then you know that feeling worthy is much more fun than feeling unworthy. If you believe you're worthy, you feel better about yourself. You see yourself starting to embody so much more. But if you command yourself to believe you're worthy, then your egoic structure is going to keep saying, "Prove it. Prove it!" Why not simply ask all of your guidance realms to show you? You've been trying so hard to overcome all beliefs. You've found it hard to justify those "New Age" belief systems, even though they seem to be so much more on track than the other taught beliefs. "So that's where the struggle has been coming from," you say. "It's the struggle with beliefs of any kind." And that nudging, the guidance and clarity you've been sensing feels so accurate. You realize that you can continue to trust because this really is a new beginning point. You simply ask to embody the true You, and to communicate this truth beyond the world's standard perceptions.

Clarity continues to grow for you: "This nudging got me here, got me so much further with the absence of work and absence of processing. What a whole new journey this is! Because remember when I began to hand it over to you guys? I started having fun. So to create a new belief system is still the absence of me? Interesting! What was all the meaning put behind beliefs? The meaning was actually emotion? It was energy? That's why I kept feeling lethargic and confined even when I was supposed to be blissed off of the planet like so many other dear ones. Show me further."

You realize that you have been engaged in a battle. This is the battle between the egoic structure that has been given such great power and the subtle, yet powerful presence of the nudging. The ego has had the power to be a life force of consciousness. This is the battle between your ego and your heart.

So much has changed because of the presence of your guides! The mind can now actually be your friend. It's the pure translator that absorbs and filters information for you to operate in a body on a planet. It really has served you very well, especially in the work place, solving equations, formulas, and otherwise. But then another question comes up from the archangelic realms, from Archangel Michael: "What would happen if you let go of the egoic approaches? What would happen if you let the formulas come from you?"

"That's a little bit different," you say. "I went through all these scholastic approaches; I studied for this, and studied for that, got this diploma, and that degree, and got credibility all over the place. So you're telling me that was about the egoic structure? What's all this ego been about? Was it to prove myself worthy to my father, my mother, to society?" Now when you ask yourself, "What's important?" something begins to resonate. Can you remember that no matter what you did in this world, it would never allow you to fully embody your essence? It would never quite fill the absence of You. And now do you see that you are becoming the true You?

Now that this clarity is presenting, you say, "Michael, thank you dear friend for showing me that these endeavors now seem so unimportant—because I am now becoming who I truly am and evolving into my higher self. Yet I can still enjoy all that I have accomplished immensely. If I would have continued to contemplate from my mind level how to gain the world's approval, it wouldn't have made me feel important. I never would have begun to live. I know you've been nudging me since childhood. Thank you. I love these colorful reminders. Will you show me more?"

And the voices reply, "Remember we are here to support you side by side. We'll always be here for you, as you have been feeling this great entourage with you everywhere you go. You can go further beyond with us, side by side. And what a brilliant gift that You are giving us! You are expanding, moving up another rung on the ladder of divinity and vibratory levels. And that is a cause for our celebration, and for celebration throughout the Universe. Great Job!" And now Yeshua asks, "Can you remember a time from your childhood, a time that you were open, a time where you had an impact? Did you realize that you had so much happening within you and so much expansion from you?"

You respond: "Yeshua do you mean you've been here the whole time? So is that the heartfelt communion we had? Was I being the instrument and being instrumental at the same time? But how can that be? I fully and completely loved it. I mean, I was awestruck by how pure and innocent I felt, and so was everyone else. Now that you bring this up, I <u>did</u> feel something of a communion—like the times when I wished for rain and it rained. I'm starting to have these memories, some as simple as playing with a dog and having the adults join in the magic and joy of playfulness and lightness. That doesn't feel like ego anymore. That feels like the love that I am beginning to remember."

You continue: "I am becoming aware of so many things. The one next to me at work, for example, the feminine structure that I've just begun to notice. You mean I've actually been showing her what a true male can really be like—from a neutrality state, an embodiment state, even though I never talked to her? Yeshua, what do you mean when you tell me that I made the difference in her life? I'm starting to get it further. With the assistance of my guidance realms, I've showed her what is possible. I've begun to open her heart, and she has begun another journey. And all of this has taken place just because I've let myself begin to remember, to embrace and embody who I am. And it just continues and continues. You mean there's no end to this?" There's no end, and yet there's continual opening. "So now, I can be in communion with you, with Michael, with all my guidance realms twenty-four hours a day?

"Well thank you, Yeshua, it's been the oddest thing," you say. "I've begun feeling at home everywhere. Now I feel more a part of the world than ever before, because everything's working without trying. I see that everyone can do this too, within their own uniquedness, the uniquedness of love that they present to everyone; and this is happening all around the planet, the Universe, and even beyond this Universe. So Yeshua, Michael, all the angelic and archangelic realms—have you been nudging everyone? It amazes me that some dear brothers still aren't listening to their own Beingness. Can I assist them too? How can I assist them to follow their hearts and open to all that is available for them?"

And Yeshua replies, "Look at a child, or look at the one who sits next to you at work; look at all of the life streams that they're going to be affecting. You are the instrument they have been wanting and asking for, actually pleading for in their dark hours, in their times of being misunderstood and misinterpreted."

"Now I'm beginning to feel so great, so natural. You're right, Yeshua—there is no ego involved, and oddly enough, there's never been a specific intention and agenda within it," you acknowledge. "As a matter of fact I'm not attracting anything; I'm expressing everything just by being in the presence, being the love, the uniquedness, the Creator Incarnate that I am. Now, let the day present. Now I can't wait to get up in the morning. I have hardly eaten this whole week, and have barely even contemplated it, but yet, the body is more vibrant than ever, just because I am walking my walk. I've heard that so many times. By walking my own walk, my whole world will open up and fall into place—physically, mentally, in every way and on every level of creation. And now that I've seen that this is real, nothing will ever be the same again!"

MEDITATION ON YOUR ANGELIC, ARCHANGELIC, AND ASCENDED HOST REALMS

You may wish to have someone read this meditation to you or record yourself reading it so you can follow along easily. Also, you can do these meditations with or without closing your eyes and over time you may experience that there is no need to close your eyes at all.

One thing that you want to do
is bring your consciousness
right through your diaphragm
beginning to let the area warm up
and open up
bringing your consciousness from the solar plexus,
diaphragm area
down through your hip bones
all the way through your upper legs
lower legs
your feet
beginning to let the areas warm up
letting them reawaken
and bringing your consciousness from the feet
all the way through the solar plexus diaphragm area
again

all the way through your crown chakra level vortex
all the way through your pineal and pituitary glands
through your throat chakra level vortex
bring your higher levels down through your heart
level
and let's begin welcoming forth
those that have been around us
Yeshua ben Joseph
the arch angelic realms of Michael
Germaine
Bartholomew
the Magdalenes
the mother Mary
lets bring forth all of these dear ones that have been
around us
and let's let your eyes go out of focus for a moment
let's ask them to let their presence be known
until we start to see across the room
a fuzzy object
and let it become fuzzier
and fuzzier
and fuzzier
with your eyes out of focus
as the presentation begins to take place
can you see the figure across the room
without thinking
let's ask them their names
what's the first name that comes to mind
what's the first name that you feel throughout every
particle of your being
let's ask them to come closer
let's ask them to let their presence be further known

let's ask them to share with us
what they have to share with us
what is the first word
or the first message
that comes to mind
the first idea
that comes to mind
and what is it that they are wanting to share with you
is it that you are so beloved
just as you are
is it a greeting that you go to with great love
is it they honor you with great love
ask them
how best can we dance together
how best can we further our communication
and complement one another
what is it that we can give to one another
whether it be pearls of wisdom
whether it be camaraderie
support
feeling one anothers presence
side by side
whether it be the comfortability that you are not
alone
whether it be the brilliance that you emanate
together
whatever it may be
let's welcome them forward
to further show themselves
to expose themselves
let's begin to play with the brotherhood of creator
essence that they are

the brilliance
the beauty
the love that you're feeling now
through your physical form
the excitement
the exhilaration
the celebration
that you share
and let's ask them further
what else do you have to show me my good friends
my beloved true family
beyond the monad states of consciousness
how much would they love to share with you
how much do they have to share with you
let's ask them to let their presence be further known
the feeling of the love
the brilliance
the pricelessnes of the brotherhood
that they have so much more to offer you
as you have to offer them
let's ask them if you can stay in this state with your
eyes wide open
so why don't you take your eyes out of the fuzzy state
can you still feel them
can you still see the glimmers and the sparkles across
the room
you can ask them for confirmation
and guidance
about your life
about your life stream
you can ask them to be a part of your life stream
and ask them what it is that they have to share

they just want to let us know
that they've been here
they want to offer more
so now you can let them offer more
let's let them show you so much further
even with your eyes wide open
what is beginning to come to mind
what are the first glimpses that you are seeing
what are the first pictures you're seeing
what are the first words you're hearing
let's ask them to speak louder
so you can fully and completely understand one
another
what else is it that they are wanting you to know
how much louder are the voices becoming
what would they have you do with your work scenario
how best can they complement in the work scenario
how best can they come into the work scenario with
you
and the family scenario
enjoying one another
dancing with one another
playing with one another
so let's ask them once again
how can you turn our whole life into the beautiful
gift of love
that it's always been
beautiful gift of brilliance
that it's always been
what do they have to share with you
is it let the world be the world™
judge not dear brothers

let us show you the way
so now you're playing with true communion
with the angelic realm
with the arch angelic realm
with the ascended host realms
so let's welcome them forward continually
letting their brilliant presence continue to arise
around you
to allowing them to become more and more
pronounced
giving confirmation after confirmation
without the high hopes of visualizations
why don't you let them become real in this realm
why don't you begin to listen and to dance with them
in this realm
and watch what begins to take place in your world
you can call it miracles
or you can call it normal
natural
and that's the part that you're referring to at this time
this is the real you
and all of the innate abilities that you have
not anything to work for
not anything to earn
but everything to enjoy

You are constantly communicating with the other kingdoms, including the animal, oceanic, plant and mineral realms. As you open yourself up to these kingdoms, your communication continues to grow.

Chapter 7

COMMUNICATING WITH
ALL OF THE KINGDOMS

The final ability we're going to speak about in this book will bring you the greatest joy to recognize and acknowledge. You have the ability to communicate with all of the diverse kingdoms on this planet—whether it be the animal or oceanic realms, the plant or mineral kingdoms, You have the ability to speak to them directly and receive wisdom back from them. Even those things that you look on as inanimate objects will take on a life for you, will speak to you. I know some of you may be saying, "Why do I need this ability? What is the point of having a conversation with a dog, or a tree, or a rock? Isn't that pretty silly?" But as you explore this ability, you will notice an empathy and understanding you weren't aware of possessing. Having this knowledge will also allow you to get your mind out of the way, and you will begin to live more through your heart center. In fact, the ability to communicate with all the kingdoms will eventually become as important to you as any of the other abilities you possess.

Every dense matter principle on this planet is made up of particles of light—whether it be the plant kingdom, the mineral kingdom, the oceanic realms, the animal kingdom or brother humanity. Everything—every cell, every atom—is made up of living consciousness that takes on a dense form, becomes a solidified structure of live consciousness presenting and projecting itself. I've spoken before about your natural innate abilities, states in which everything that has always been yours is available. These levels that you're beginning to embody are opening now because there is no longer the same filtration of the mind. Everything from facilitation with other dear ones, to speaking with the consciousness of objects, to letting those objects begin to communicate with you—there are truly so many abilities you have that you are now discovering as you give yourself permission to explore your uniquedness. There is truly no end to what you can and will experience. And much of this opening has to do with recognizing that everything on this planet, and the planet itself, is made up of living consciousness.

Communicating with other kingdoms really frees you, because now you're not preoccupied by the mind. If you let go of the "I should, I ought, I must, I have to," and all the rest of the chatter for a minute, everything can completely open up to be enjoyed more than ever. You are in a state of listening to the world, rather than listening to what the mind says about the world. This is really like the childhood scenario. When you watch children playing, you notice that they're simply being offspring, simply having a blast in every way with nothing preoccupying them. They're not concerned about tomorrow, the next day, the day after that, six months to a year from now, their educational preferences or anything else. What they're focused on is exactly what's before them. And the reason why they're only focused on what's before them is because they know that nothing else really matters, nor is anything real until it's presenting right in front of them. That childlike state is your natural state. Being open to everything, truly being able to experience and enjoy all of the most brilliant gifts that are right before you, allows you to see beyond the tunnel vision—beyond being attached to a future outcome. You are beyond focus but completely expressing.

The planetary grid system is a web of magnetics that holds together the solidified structure of the earth. As a live deity, the earth has always possessed its own grid system, no different from the karmic grid system that affected everyone's physicality. But as humanity arises, the earth is arising as well, and now everything on the planet is constantly changing, shifting, opening. There are universal magnetic changes occurring at the level of the planetary grid system; all of the elements are beginning to re-arise as all of the kingdoms are re-arising. In the same way that the karmic grid system kept everything "stable" for eons, the planetary grid system has been a brilliant crutch, an absolutely solidified state that has held all of the cavities and templates of the planet in place. No matter where humanity has gone, this planetary grid has held humanity in place and supported it. And now the planetary grid system is fully coming to life, going through magnetic re-infusions of light.

There is a planetary Beingness I refer to that is about the planet as a whole, as a live deity, a consciousness within itself. When I talk about you in relation to this planetary Beingness, I am speaking of your ability to communicate with the planet so the planet can communicate back. As the planet loves to share all that you could ever want, contemplate or imagine, it will show you anything that you ask about, anything and everything that calls to you. Once you begin to ask the planet questions it will share with you all the mystical realms; it will share with you about the plant kingdoms, the mineral kingdoms, the oceanic realms, even the fairy kingdoms. It will share with you the underlying states of the grid system, and the caverns of creation; it will share with you the crystalline caverns underneath the oceanic realms. It will share anything and everything, because as the live deity that it is, it loves to share and support. The earth is no different from all of these kingdoms we have been playing with throughout this book and throughout all of creation. It doesn't want a battle for peace. It wants to be the peace that dissolves the battle. It wants to dance together with you.

The platelets are the ground you walk on, the planetary structures beneath us all. These platelets are the solidified structures of grid systems, based in the magnetics of holding their own resonance and frequency in place. But these platelets of magnetics are opening up to further explore and to further open up brother humanity, because these are dense structures that have been affecting your physical structures. When we speak of planetary Beingness, these are levels that you get to play with that are becoming more alive than ever, continuing to come alive to support you as you're supporting them. As humanity continues to awaken and evolve, to remember and move forward, these platelets are also beginning to change to further support and to complement you.

The magnetic grid system is a system in which the frequencies, the resonances of the planet are keeping together a solidified form. These levels are particles of consciousness that have created in a solidified form. As the planet is a living deity populated with living deities, the grid system is based in metals and minerals, based also in the water levels and nature kingdoms— creating a grid system that is called magnetics. From this buoyancy, from a molecular structure literally pulling together into the fabrication of one manifest state, ions come together to create form. It's the energetics that are holding the whole web and structure of the planet together in one fabricated solidified structure.

The planetary matrix is a matrix of gold, a matrix of light that holds the core of the planet through its magnetic structures, keeping the platelets in a certain alignment. As the consciousness of humanity is shifting, so the planetary matrix is shifting. This planetary matrix holds every memory, every experience that's ever been had through the dimensional planes on this planetary structure. It is a live deity that is created with realms of light, magnetics and crystalline structures that amplify different levels of the planet's magnetic conduits. This matrix is now re-arising and changing within itself, just as humanity is changing and rewriting itself, releasing the old memories of everything that has ever played out.

There are numerous planetary shifts taking place where the planetary matrix is re-awakening within itself. When I speak of re-awakening I'm speaking of universal shifts. The magnetics that have held this solar system together are being pulled upon due to the consciousness of humanity. In turn, these planetary shifts are affecting your consciousness through the physical format, causing your physical form to open, and open, and open, to further complement and dance with you. And as this is happening, of course, the planetary shifts are going to arise to affect your physicality, all the way to the functionability of your body principle. These shifts are affecting your thought processes and behavioral mannerisms, and the same thing is happening with all the dear brothers around you.

As the planetary matrix shifts, it's bringing all the old archaic debris up and to the forefront to be dissolved. This psychic debris is not, never was, and never will be You. There is a mighty shift that is taking place within this planet. And because everyone and everything is connected, every particle of consciousness is affected. For example, as the mass consciousness is dissolving, it is changing over the weather patterns. Although many have called this global warming, it isn't global warming, but rather a shifting of planetary magnetics; it's the shifting of the consciousness of brother humanity to re-awaken and re-open as who they are, to run so much further. And as these planetary shifts take place, please be open. Please be available. These shifts are occurring to further complement and support You, your physicality, and your mind level. The dissolvement of archaic emotional debris is freeing you to be fully and completely wide awake and alert once again as Creator Incarnate.

Planetary structures are continuing to realign, rebuild and regenerate themselves. Through these planetary structures we're working and playing with the continental belts that are the earth's platelets. We're actually playing with the core of the planet itself. For these structures that are right there before you, are all becoming exposed, becoming wide open again; all of it is coming into a state of accessibility. The clarities and the tools that are there, that have always been there, are re-arising to support and comfort and dance with you. As you're giving to these planetary structures, as you're giving love, as you're honoring and acknowledging the divinity of it all, you're helping to re-stabilize the energy and life Beingness.

Now we are playing with all of the kingdoms. You see, when I'm out in the yard walking around, I'm not looking for anything. It's just like what we were speaking of in other chapters about being completely wide open to All That Is. When you communicate with the other kingdoms, you are going beyond the constructs of illusions, beyond the constructs of perceptional realities and perceptional beliefs that you have been taught. You don't have one specific intention, one specific focus or direction. Instead you're letting everything come to you. So why does it matter whether or not you have an intention? When you're looking, when you have an intention, you start to get engaged, creating tunnel vision. On the other hand, when you let everything start to present, you're letting it share its beauty, its ambience, its creativity. And all the messages—even beyond messages—all the clarities and communication you receive, whether they come from a puppy dog or kitty cat, a lion, tiger, or giraffe; whether they come from a plant or the stucco on your home or your furniture, they are all going to share everything, all the way to their first origination point.

So why not try this experiment? When you're sitting and looking at the plants in your garden, simply watch how the plant kingdom will begin presenting and emanating its own essence and its own presence for you. A plant may share that its minerals are a little bit low, or that everything's right on track. It's honoring you as you simply let it be, let it continue to share its own pollination levels all the way to where the plant came from. And it is ready to share about how it became a plant, out of pure consciousness, how it began. When there was once a tiny particle of consciousness, a seed, the vibrancy of the particles of consciousness in the air caused it to be blown into the brilliant atmospheric realms, to make a landing point in the field. There a plant sprang from the seed and started to grow wild. And the plant continued to prosper, to be expanded upon with new seeds, letting itself become much more plentiful, until the day that one of those new seeds sprang up to become the plant in your own garden.

What about the mineral kingdom that makes up the soil where the plant lives? We know that the minerals upon the planet are here to sustain life, just as we know that the planetary mineral matrix continues to metamorphosize and change. The plant honors the mineral matrix for the beautiful consciousness that it is. It's an honoring of the planetary mineral matrix as it holds all of the soil and the dirt in place, and also the plant and soil in a communion with one complementing the other. Now all of this is what the plant is showing you right now. And it speaks to you, saying, "I want a little more water and some added minerals, please. Then watch me flourish even that much further." These kingdoms constantly want to honor you with their presence. And as you are also being honored by their presence, they are being honored by your accepting their communicative states, by your ability to accept the information and the data to prosper and complement all concerned.

You know, I have to chuckle about how the mind can creep in, trying to take over—because that's when you're starting to judge that the garden is a good garden, a bad garden, a fertile garden, a garden that won't grow, rather than seeing and experiencing the garden for what it is. You judge the garden rather than letting the truth become exposed to you, the truth which will offer so much more clarity, which will give you the ability to let yourself be clear and more accessible to play within a whole new world.

What if I told you that what serves the kingdoms is to let the garden go where it goes? You can be assisting it by using soil additives or whatever the ground and plants are asking for, rather than giving your mind the power. You see, you're not making this about you, which is the first tendency of the mind level. Remember that the mind level has been taught to make <u>everything</u> about that little you, creating a false sense of self-importance. What happens when you make something not about yourself? What do you do when you start to judge it as a bad garden or good garden in the same way that you define a person as bad or good? As the Creator that you are, what you're doing when you make such a judgment is commanding it so. You are commanding it into a reality. So at least in your world, the garden becomes good or bad, just as the person becomes good or bad. By this point you've already started to close yourself off. And it's like putting a rock or a pebble in a river, eventually it's going to create a dam. Even that single pebble creates an obstruction that the water is forced to go around. As we honor the gardens that we were playing with, the roses, the trees, as we honor the dear ones who are neither good or bad, we're playing with the planetary structure. We're playing with their presences and their brilliant diversities, bringing these areas further to life, letting them give back to you again as a brotherhood, as a camaraderie in a mutual dance that you're having together.

So if you're sitting in your garden looking at your beautiful violets, or your tropical hibiscus, or your spiny cacti, be open to what they're presenting. Because your mind level is not in control, they can actually begin presenting themselves exponentially to you, as you simply enjoy their radiating beauty. Your enjoyment is automatically going to assist them to bloom further, assist You to bloom further, because it's a mutual honoring. Now you are absolutely neutral with the garden. You are fully, completely allowing yourself to enjoy it. And when you're right here playing with the plant kingdom, you've automatically let the business take care of the business, let the accounts take care of the accounts, let the body be the body, and you're no longer affected by these things. You're no longer engaged with all of these cyclical cycles that no longer complement.

Now through this communication and appreciation of all the kingdoms, true enjoyment is beginning to present, whether it be business agreements, whether it be finances or other paperwork, whether it be relationships with offspring or the animal kingdom. It's a mutual honoring all the way through, not an attempt to honor, not an attempt to do or be something. You'll simply continue to enjoy your own presence, letting yourself enjoy every particle of creation as it was created to be, and also allowing for it to communicate back. A flower is not just a flower any longer. The radiance and divinity of all the world loves, loves, loves to present its beauty for all of humanity. It is there not to be merely glanced upon or bypassed, but to be fully and completely embraced. Remember—the flower isn't trying. The flower is actually emanating its own presence to you through its elegance, uniquedness, divinity, just as you're emanating your presence to the flower. And once again, you're not focused on the plant kingdom, you're simply letting it communicate while you expand exponentially.

Let's take a cup of coffee, for example. When you're open, a cup of coffee will show you its first origination point, from the moment the seed was planted in the ground. It will share how it grew and was carefully tended; it will show you the dear brothers who tended to it; show you how it flowered and then bore the coffee beans. It will tell you how those beans were harvested by the dear brothers in the field, and how it was roasted by other dear ones, and on, and on, through all the events along its journey. You can instantly know all the coffee's history, up to the moment that it came to be there in your cup.

That simple beverage wants to share its journey with you because it loves the communion and playing together. Now, let me be clear: If every time you poured a cup of coffee it shared its entire history with you, this could easily become very distracting. But the coffee's story is not meant as a distraction. It is simply there to show you the link that exists between you and every particle of consciousness in this world, the brilliant diversities of all the particles, all the consciousness of this planet. I'm very used to it, so I don't let my coffee's story disturb me. It's like a song playing in the background of my day, merely creating richness, adding to the day and amplifying it.

This brings me to the question of purpose within the kingdoms. I don't feel guilty when I drink my coffee, even though I know it has a consciousness. But what about animals? What about the animal and oceanic kingdoms? I have had dear ones tell me they are vegetarian or vegan because they wish to eat only live food. They tell me that they're certainly not going to enjoy the flesh of any animal because they would be eating the fear of a dear brother who has been forcibly removed from the planet. Of course, I honor vegetarians and vegans. However, there are lots of perceptional beliefs here. Some of these dear ones may be salivating over a filet mignon, but feel they can't eat one because steaks are full of fear. Or out of great love they ask me how they could possibly eat another living being. "Wouldn't that be like murder?" they ask. "Wouldn't eating an animal be supporting a terrible behavior?"

Let me be very clear: There is nothing dishonorable about eating animal flesh, because you're honoring the dear brother who gave his physicality to honor you. That's one of the reasons the animal kingdom has been here through the eons. Beyond assisting and holding the planetary matrix intact and in alignment, there are dear brothers that have been here to provide sustenance and a mutual honoring. What if you begin to let yourself honor the dear brothers who are ready to give their physicality for your health and vitality and wholeness?

Now we're talking about true reality. Now we're talking about true divinity. Now we're talking about complete ecological nature and much more. So, if you do not ever eat the beef, or the chicken, or the fishes because you think it's a "sin." What a dishonor it would be for yourself and everyone else, including the planetary matrix. If no one eats the salmon, how many salmon can be on a planet at one time? How many beautiful, beautiful animals can be on the planet at one time? Now one thing I want to say though, there are many different ways of honoring this kingdom.

In an earlier chapter I spoke about the first time I ever tasted fish, when my angel Mary and I had our first feast together. At our beautiful dinner communion I actually <u>experienced</u> the fish. We were sitting at the table, about to partake in this beautiful delicate gourmet feast, and the fish we were about to partake in was presenting itself to me. So what did I experience? I was presented with being in a stream with this same fish. This may seem to you like it would be a strange and possibly uncomfortable feeling. But it was really quite fun and natural. It was a way of showing my appreciation to this dear brother for participating in the beautiful feast we were about to have. To acknowledge him futher, I said, "Thank you so much for offering your physicality for our complete, exquisite enjoyment. Namaste, dear brother!" Now some of you may feel that was insensitive of me to partake in the flesh of another. But hear me when I share with you, this salmon was delighted to offer himself. He knew it was a beautiful celebration, and was honored by the part he was to play.

So partake of the animal kingdom and the oceanic realms without guilt or fear, knowing that you are NOT supporting the behavioral mannerisms from a sex, power, and greed dynamic. Of course, some dear brothers have chosen to make these large corporate businesses out of the animal kingdom that are based on greed. This seems so dominant and unnecessary. But what's truly happening now is that doors and opportunities are starting to be closed because of their behaviors, because of the way they have been dishonoring the kingdoms. In their greed they have dishonored ecological balance, the true passion and true essence of the cyclical journey. And now these businesses are being closed down due to the lack of integrity involved with turning the kingdoms into a cash game rather than an honoring game. As that's taking place you're going to assist in raising the vibratory levels, bringing that kingdom up to the forefront to be noticed, to be assisted and treated with honor. And you do this, not by creating a battle for peace, but by being the peace that dissolves the battle.

Are the animal and oceanic kingdoms who live with us more for companionship or sustenance? I know that some of you may ask, "What's the difference? An animal is an animal. If I eat a cow, then why not eat a kitty cat or a puppy?" Well, why not? There are places in this world where dear brothers do eat kitty cats, puppies, and even insects. And my answer is still the same: These dear ones give themselves for sustenance in a mutual honoring. Once again, there is a divine order at work. There are so many facets to the animal kingdom. Some have come to the planet to walk with you side by side, to offer you support, communion, and camaraderie. Others, like some of the oceanic realms, have come to play with DNA and the planetary platelets. And some have come to offer their physicality for sustenance, just as they offer their feces to revitalize the planetary matrix and the mineral kingdom. This whole kingdom is constantly giving and receiving. All these creatures, uniquedly, have their own journeys, and you can communicate with each of them.

Here comes my kitty cat, Snickerdoodle, who shares with me, "I'm a little bit low on iron today. If we have some blended tuna and a little Pedialite water, it's going to let everything be re-calculated to realign itself." Then he shares what's going on when I'm home, when I'm not home, how his brother chased him, or how his sister ate all the food in his bowl. He shares what's going on in the animal kingdom as a whole, and in his personal incarnational journeys as well—

revealing all the times he has presented in a physical-ity. He communicates with me about the Pleiadians, the light beings who are around the property, and how he gets to play and communicate with them, too. We get to celebrate and enjoy the beautiful heartfelt com-munion that we share, and I get to assist so brilliantly as a conduit. I get to assist so brilliantly in opening his heart, showing him how loved and lovable he is. What an honoring it is for him to purr and stroke my physicality, just as I get to stroke his. What I'm really doing here is opening up all the portals within his own Beingness—letting him come back through the heart again in equality and honor, which is also allowing his organs to begin rebuilding, and letting his life stream begin to re-open.

Then there are the red and gold koi fish at our home whose lives are spent swimming in our pond. These brothers are not forcibly detained. They want to be here. And I ask you, how could you really own one of any kingdom when they are a life force within them-selves with a journey of their own? Although the voices of the koi fish are different from Snickerdoodle's, they still commune with me and present information. They share with me how much they love the heat of the sun. They tell me when they're ready for some tetra food and perhaps their water could be just a bit fresher. Our kitty cat Riley, our Lion King, used to visit them each day before he left the planet. He would watch them swimming in circles. They would come up to the surface of the water to greet him. Such a benevolent communion was always taking place between these supposed enemies. And on the day before he left the planet, Riley went out to make his goodbyes to them. His ashes are nourishing a plant in the garden nearby. Many times these oceanic brothers have presented that their dear Riley is still here around the pond, still communing with them from another dimension.

Now we come to a facet of this ability that many dear brothers may not understand or take to be important. Since all things in this world are made up of particles of consciousness, inanimate objects have their own consciousness. They are communicating with you as well. I know this may seem a bit out there to some of you. You may have found my story about a living cup of coffee to be somewhat out there, somewhat ungrounded. However, once you realize that all consciousness is communicating, you'll notice it all the time. For example, I'll be walking outside on the patio and the barbecue is emanating its presence, "Hey, Will, it sounds like fun to play with you today! Thanks." The barbecue is also communicating that this would be a wonderful night for a romantic dinner with my bride, or with wonderful friends. As we're preparing dinner, playing with the barbecue, enjoying all the tools and toys, it becomes an honor for all concerned.

Then at the same time I'm hearing from the stucco on our home, all the beauty that the consciousness of the stucco is wanting to share about itself. It tells me how and when it was put up, and shares about the underlying structure beneath it. The stucco presents where it's cracking, where things are breaking down a bit in the structure level, and why it's cracking. It shares where it came from, all the way to the rock levels, telling me that some of the rocks came from

San Jose, California, and some from the southern regions. The stucco presents where those rocks were first found, sharing when they were first exposed and then broken up by the machines. It shares about all the dear brothers who were involved in bringing that stucco all the way to our home, and all the blessedness for the dear ones involved. It tells me about the dear ones who applied the stucco, and how fully and completely they were loving the job, having a blast with it and with their own beautiful expressions of creativity.

And simultaneously, the stucco presents what a joy it is to watch the weather patterns of the planet, to watch all the flowering of the plant kingdoms, the prosperity of growth, the beautiful kitty cats who wander by, who rub against its surface. It may not be easy to become used to this notion of the different kingdoms. And some of you may really have difficulty listening to things, like the stucco on the walls, to believe that there is as much life in the piece of concrete as in an animal. But once you understand that all creatures and things are just different levels of consciousness, it becomes so much easier to hear them. I just let myself simply be open to all of creation being vibrantly alive. Isn't it simply amazing that we are all this live consciousness that loves to share about itself?

Within all the brilliance of creation, these kingdoms and objects want to share. Let's return to that cup of coffee I spoke of earlier. I have so much fun with this. When I was at the coffee shop this morning and picked up my cup, it was so beautiful. I had it right there in my hand, and as I started to drink, I let the coffee share what it had to share as the live deity that it was. Actually it first presented as a live deity being consumed through my physicality. So, automatically, without a perceptional judgment, I instantly became the coffee looking out of the coffee cup as the tiny little particles of consciousness that it was—looking at my physicality, at my tiny little particles. And I was the coffee moving down through my esophagus, all the way through my abdomen, through the liver levels and through the rest of the systems for processing.

But more importantly than that, the coffee was also presenting the beautiful consciousness that it was. It shared where it was originally planted and what all of the dear brothers were going through, and where everyone was on their own personal journey. It shared when it began to be harvested and all of the dear brothers that were involved with that experience. It even shared how it was sent to this continent, to the factories for the roasting, etc., and all of the dear brothers presented in that creation as well.

I saw everything, right down to the makers of the coffee mugs, and saw how all of these life streams came together all the way to that one little store, so that I could be blessed and honored to partake in it. Now I could say that $3.84 is a little much to pay for a single cup of coffee, and I would be correct. But somehow when the coffee is sharing with me all of the dear ones who were a part of its journey, $3.84 is really nothing in comparison. Now I can fully and completely enjoy the coffee, knowing the brilliance and gift that it is. Once I'm open and looking at the whole, I can let myself fully and completely enjoy and celebrate it along with everyone involved in its making.

As I partake, I'm also blessing all of the dear ones who were a part of that corporation, all of the dynamics that one cup of coffee went through to be placed right in my hand. I'm actually assisting them, not just by giving my $3.84 worth of abundance, but by understanding and celebrating the love and enjoyment of all who contributed to it. Now other doors are opening up all over the place around me in my own personal life because I made that investment. I invested in them. I invested in myself. I certainly wasn't going to hold myself back from something that I love for a mere $3.84. And I'm certainly not going to sit here and go back and forth from a perceptional judgment about the "overpricing" of this or that. I simply ask myself, "Do I want the coffee or not?" If I do, so be it. Bring it on. And, I'm going to have a blast drinking that delicious coffee.

Some of you are wondering if I would pay $8.00 for a gallon of gasoline. If gasoline cost $8.00 a gallon, I would either buy it or not. If I decided to buy it, that's fabulous, because I'm going to enjoy it. And just as with the example of the coffee, I'm also going to be enjoying all of the dear brothers who were a part of it, those who worked to locate the petroleum, and refine it, and get it all the way to the pump. Hear me when I say I will enjoy all the brilliant blessedness that is, to have all of those gifts and the ability to drive a car vehicle. Now, because of all the work these dear brothers went through to bring this right before me, I can drive my car vehicle.

Of course, I could sit back and start to create a lot of perceptional judgments and dramas about the price, but I have so much more that I can be playing with. I'm certainly not going to separate or polarize myself due to the consciousness of what's going on globally. Why should I when I can simply have a blast seeing through the perceptional judgments and idle complaints? Whoever said that I have to purchase gas in the first place? Whoever said I could not let my physicality do the work, and walk here, or walk there, or take public transportation? Do you see? I have all of these options still, and now I can just enjoy the purchasing of this beautiful gasoline. What a blessing it is to have it right here before me! Not because I have to purchase it, but because I can, and how blessed I am. I made that investment to be able to enjoy driving my car vehicle. And because of that investment, look at all of these other opportunities opening up. Look at all these other kingdoms beginning to share themselves because I'm not so polarized, so shut down, so focused on a tiny little pinpoint of expression, putting all of this energy into the price. I'm just going to enjoy driving. I am now truly more abundant than ever. The purity and clarity is freedom.

What are we heading toward once we recognize that everything has a consciousness, that there's consciousness in the tiniest particle? What does that mean to us as humanity? Contemplate the animals around you, the plants around you, everything around you having consciousness. Then contemplate exactly what that will do for your consciousness. Everything will metamorphosize into a harmonious state because we're all here to celebrate one another. We're all here to celebrate our creation, all here to experience and explore our creation, all here to play with our creation. This is not from a dominance of power, or from the phantom called the ego that says, "I'm more powerful or more important than you."

This is not just about our love for the different kingdoms; it's just simply about enjoying them, and enjoying yourself. If you've noticed, none of this communion is about trying anymore; none of it is about becoming constrained. You're now open to everything. Now, I must be clear here: You're not going to focus on the garden, not going to focus on this certain plant for what it wants or needs. You're not going to focus on the rocks or the stucco, or barbecue, or the lounge chairs. You're simply letting them present. And as you do this, you no longer have tunnel vision that causes you to feel so confined, not putting all of this "I think, I should, I ought, I must, I have to, I need to" energy into your world. By avoiding all of these rules and repetitive states of how it has to be, can and can't be, you are letting yourself be open to enjoy and experience true clarity.

This is going full circle back to the dissolvement of perceptional judgments of What Is. Now you're going to experience one thing today, and then tomorrow another unfoldment is going to present. And I promise you, you're not going to use a backed-up archived memory, a back-up of emotionally-driven beliefs and experiences. You're not going to say, "Been there, done that. This took place and that took place." You're going to experience each unfoldment from a whole different state because now you're not putting anything into it. I want to honor where brother humanity has been. But now when you step into the world, you're no longer being run by a time continuum or trying to learn your lessons and come to this realization. You're just going to let it all come to the forefront to be enjoyed. And I promise, you will be handling different situations in eons of different ways because you're playing with what's presenting. As there are no longer old archaic perceptions based in experiences that created belief in judgments of good or bad. You become free to go beyond it, to see the truth of What Is and receive complete clarity.

You're going to begin to truly experience, and you're going to have a blast. And every time you experience something it can be so much different, because you're not trying to create a certain way of doing something or a certain experience. You're letting the experiences create themselves. You are getting to dance right through them. This way, you can let all kingdoms present themselves, learning what they're asking for— whatever it may be.

As you continue to let yourself be open, all sorts of information, data and memories will begin to arise. So let's break it down into dimensions. How much curiosity do you have? How could certain events have happened in the prehistoric age? Well, dear heart, you lived through the prehistoric age; this is when you first started playing in a body on a planet, playing with evolution. You have been watching the changes going on from the first period of humanity. You have seen the progression and the evolvement of humanity, and the planet, and the whole Universe. This evolvement is what is happening right now, more intensely than ever right now, because humanity has been asking and is now ready to welcome the changes. Even beyond the physical traits that are changing, the outside world is changing over, expanding through the different kingdoms that are all so brilliantly re-harmonizing themselves into a mutual honoring. This is all because you as Creator said, "I cannot have one certain level of creation out of resonance with the rest. I, as Creator, command all kingdoms into a harmonious state." We're all here to celebrate one another, to celebrate our creation. We are all here to experience our creation. We're all here to play with our creation.

MEDITATION ON COMMUNICATING WITH ALL OF THE KINGDOMS

You may wish to have someone read this meditation to you or record yourself reading it so you can follow along easily. Also, you can do these meditations with or without closing your eyes and over time you may experience that there is no need to close your eyes at all.

What you want to do here is to bring your
consciousness
right through your torso
right through your heart
letting the energy in that area
the consciousness
the expandedness
begin to open through the heart chakra level vortex
in the front and the back
letting the energy continue to grow
bringing your consciousness
up through your throat
through your pineal and pituitary glands
through your crown chakra level vortex
all the way down your arms
your upper arms
your lower arms

out your hands
down through your abdomen
your solar plexus levels
all the way down through your gender principle
down your upper legs
your lower legs
and out the bottom of your feet
now that you're in a clear state of consciousness
let's bring forth any state of the animal species
lion, tiger, puppy dog, kitty cat
whether it be the horsies
whether it be the oceanic realms
just bring them forward in front of you
let's ask them what they have to share with you
what would they like to show you
let's go with the first picture
the first thought
that presents for you
from them
this is these kingdoms that we have stepped out of
time to enjoy
this is these kingdoms that we have stepped out of the
mind to enjoy
using the mind now as your friend
using the mind now as a tool
as a conduit
lets let the pictures continue to grow
because now as we're watching
now as we're hearing
we're welcoming these kingdoms in to show their
omnipotence unto you
that have always been
that will always be

it's letting all of it begin to open up to a whole new
world together
let's let them take you on journeys
journeys through their species
through their kingdoms
to their burrows
and to the crystalline structures in the platelets of the
planet
let's let them begin and continue to create a camaraderie together
let's also ask them
what is it I can offer to you my good friend
are you lacking minerals
or certain supplements, elements
being that of the domestic animal kingdom
what is it they want to share with you
what is it they want to show you
what is it they want for you to hear
to see
so that we can dance together side by side
it's a brilliant connected priceless camaraderie of
connectedness
communion
freedom
let's let the love that they have to share flow right
through you
to you
from you as well
as the dance is now beginning
to play with so much further than beyond the day to
day cycles of the mind
lets let them begin to show the gift that they truly are
walking side by side as a brotherhood once again

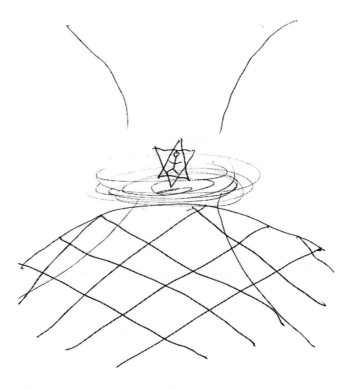

The clear state represented by the six-pointed star is a union of the higher and lower selves. When you live in this state, you are constantly open, emanating All That Is.

Chapter 8

LIVING IN A CLEAR STATE

Now we've come to the final chapter of this book. You are beginning to acknowledge your wonderful gifts as Creator Incarnate, waking up to All That Is. So where do you go from here? What lies ahead for you? This is the time to speak about what lies beyond recognizing your abilities. Living in a clear state is about acknowledging those abilities, using those abilities, and living in neutrality. This is your "I Am" presence of neutrality, openness, fluidity, and expression. It is about the freedom from obligation, responsibility, and identifications. It is about living in complete awareness and integrity, of living in the presence of movement, alignment, fruition, and creation.

Your natural state is one of "is-ness," of neutrality. You are completely wide open. Optimum health and well-being on every level of creation is yours. Your natural state is total simplicity within every level of your being—mentally, physically, from your higher levels into your outside world and beyond. Your natural state is one of fluidity, without conflict, without ailment. In this state of omnipotence that has been and is your natural birthright, lies the real You. There is total integration and integrity within every particle of your being. Everything is flowing, working, opening, and receiving. In this state of complete expansion, of clarity, purity, openness, you are entirely within your own presence, being in the world but not of it. You are living in total bliss, total joy, not embodying the world and its outside activities.

When I speak of neutrality, I am speaking of a life where the giving and the receiving become one. Neutrality is the state of no mind, no chatter, but instead the complete presence of You. Imagine throughout all of your physical presence, being in a body on a planet and being wide open to all of the elements—of the oceanic realms, the mineral and plant kingdoms, the animal kingdoms—and of course, to all of humanity. You find yourself tuning in to a higher state of consciousness, hearing the Universe, its tones and frequencies. You're no longer seeking from the mind, no longer being of the mind, which is a whole other world within itself. Once you've stopped seeking, you disengage the magnetics of your physicality from all the world. You are always yourself—not striving to please or fit in. This allows the whole world to change, to open, to accommodate and complement you twenty-four hours a day. And being in this state, whether you're at the local coffee shop, or in the corporate world, or in the midst of a carnival, there's no longer a separation. Instead there is a complete embodiment of you on every level, in all the brilliant facets of diversities going on around you. Your natural state is about being in the world, but not of it nor affected by it; letting the world revolve around you, rather than within you.

Let me be clear: You are not <u>doing</u> anything. You are simply letting the world be the world. What is this? It's letting the outside world and its sequences of events take care of themselves without becoming personally engaged. You are literally letting the whole world around you begin to change. You remember that the changes are happening to further complement you, and you need not be involved. Letting the world be the world is letting the world and its manifestations present to further complement you, rather than requiring the involvement mentally, emotionally, and physically. You simply <u>let work</u>—let the world begin to work for you, let the load be lifted and let everything begin to happen around You, for You. You are letting the angelic, archangelic and ascended host realms come into your life stream to get things moving. But once again, this is not about trying, it is about allowing.

Have you ever <u>challenged</u> yourself to be neutral? That's pretty comical, isn't it? "Okay, I'm going to be neutral," says the mind. "Ohmmmm." And then the thoughts start creeping in, one by one. "Why did he say this? Why did she do that? What did that email mean?" You get to the point where you're saying, "How long should I meditate? Am I doing it right?" When the mind catches itself, it says, "Wait, wait, wait! I have to be in the state of the Ohmmmm!" And the whole process starts all over again. Now I'm not criticizing meditation. It is a wonderful tool to use on your journey. Meditation is about finding a linear state, bypassing the ego mind. But that's where you may find yourself trying to force the issue again. In a sense, you are <u>using</u> your ego to have no ego. If you simply say, "I choose to know the truth. Show me the overview," you have suddenly bypassed that little mind. It may seem as though you're putting yourself into a choice scenario again, but in truth you're going beyond choice. You're going into remembrance. This is because you have decided to re-examine who you truly are from a disengaged state, to know where the thought forms arise.

There are really two types of embodiment. There is the embodiment of the world, and there is the embodiment of your higher levels. We know the embodiment of the world all too well. It is the embodiment of the ego, the "I think, I should, I ought, I must," that drives so many dear ones crazy! This type of embodiment says, "I am never good enough. I will never be good enough." This type of embodiment is completely and totally engaged. It can never be anything else. But then there is the other type of embodiment.

When I ask you to embody your higher levels, I am asking you to let the heart that you are, the love that you are, the divinity that you are, the facet of Creator that you are, begin to speak to you, steer you, and journey you. This is the embodying of love, brilliance, divinity, and presence. But beyond that, it's the embodiment of the higher through the lower, the Universe through the physical, the alpha and the omega becoming one, taking command of every particle of your being. This is about following the nudges, following the voice that is right there within you, around you, letting your higher levels give to you.

Some may say, "But I can't go live in a monastery on a mountaintop! I have to go to work every day, and make a living, and live in the real world!" This is precisely what I mean about being in the world but not of it. You don't have to live on a mountaintop, ohming your life away. You can go to work, see your family, watch the evening news—even vote in elections—and still feel neutrality. You are not giving your power away. You are not living in an unreal world. For the first time, you are living in the real one.

This embodiment is all of You, from the higher to the lower, coming right through the physical. Fully and completely, from the bottom of your feet, all the way through your heart level and up through your crown chakra level of consciousness, you're beginning to embody your higher levels. I call this welcoming in your big guns. Because now you allow your guidance realms to take command of your soul, your life, your work, your wealth, your mind, your body, your world, and every particle of your being. Do you remember when we spoke of the dear one who took a new way home one day and met her true love? What did she do, if not simply let the world be the world? There was no work. There was no struggle, no manifesting, no attempting to manifest or shape a destiny. She was just walking through the world, embodying all of creation. In that state of fluidity, everything was open and available to her.

The fluid state is about moving right through creation, through every circumstance, every situation, every scenario, being able to dance with it, to be in it, not of it. There is continual motion, through the prosperity, through the finances, through the family monads, through relationships, through every level of creation. Can you imagine being in this incredible diversity, playing with it, dancing with it, expressing through it, and enjoying your natural state without the world imploding on you? In this state, you're expressing through the world, making your mark in the world without work. It's just you showing up, being yourself, without the embodiment of others and the power given to others. What is this state, but you in your true power, true love that is expressing in every way, on every level, and every scenario? When you've let the world become real, you've eliminated the stagnation which is created by constantly recycled ideals, constant judgments. The real world is a playground, an Eden to be enjoyed, to be celebrated, to be exquisitely embodied and embraced.

Remember when we spoke of road rage? By letting go of emotion you let go of the rage. When this happens you don't struggle to forgive or understand what other dear brothers are doing. You simply relax into your fully integrated state. If you were to get the mind involved, you could easily start reflecting back more rage. You could feel picked on, powerless, frightened, and become super aggressive. You are filled with emotion, out of control. By letting go of emotion, by relaxing into an integrated state, you find that real world. I'm not suggesting that you go off into some Lala Land. Letting go of emotion and connecting with your higher levels doesn't mean that you forget how to drive or opt out of anything. No, instead you are more capable than ever. Your mind is no longer engaged.

As you are now beginning to reactivate and use the mind as at tool, you might begin by giving it the complementary job of addressing your higher levels. Remember that the mind is your friend, and it is learning how to channel those guidance realms. So you might say, "Thank you higher levels. You know, I almost got wrapped up in that ego thing again. But oh, thank you, because I want to know so much more. I want to remember so much more. And I don't want to fight to have my freedom." The mind begins to recognize that throughout all of the perceptual time continuum, the histories and otherwise, there's always been that fight, the fight to be free, the fight to be different. You are learning that being <u>of</u> the world means always fighting, and the biggest fight is the fight to be the same as everyone else.

Look to your guidance levels to see the truth. Sometimes it isn't so obvious. And sometimes, things that helped you on your journey before now only seem to slow you down. For example, how many of you create a fight for peace? The idea behind these words is completely brilliant. The heartfelt desire behind them has been completely priceless. But what about the <u>meaning</u> behind the words? Fighting for peace doesn't seem very peaceful does it? Since this "fight" has always been more about remembering your own essence and divinity—a wake-up call—now you are able to give up the fight entirely. Instead you become the peace that dissolves the battle.

In other words, you're not <u>trying</u> to be peaceful. You're not <u>trying</u> to create peace. You're not <u>trying</u> to be the difference in the world. What if you were to cease trying and just let everything be neutral? "Oh no!" says the mind level. "If I let myself be neutral, what's going to happen? Isn't that giving up?" So you want to end war, and you find yourself at a peace demonstration. Everyone around you wants peace, yet they are so angry about war, the air is thick with violence. You ask yourself, "Am I trying to force change? Am I meeting force with force?" Then you let your higher levels take over, and in neutrality, truly in peace, you begin to create peace.

Now you're stepping into a whole new world. You're stepping out of the world that was running you, with its time clocks, calendars, identifications, emotions, and all of the taught behavioral mannerisms of survival. Let me back up a bit and say that you will still probably need a clock and a calendar! But they will simply be there to tell you the time, not to cause guilt or anxiety, not to dictate your life any longer. When you examine your old world you ask yourself, "What has all of this stuff been about anyway?" You wonder why you thought you would have to find a partner by a certain age, or why you had to have one who looked a certain way or had a certain type of job. You wonder why you thought employment had to be drudgery. You seem to recall thinking that you had to have a certain amount of cash to be happy. You wonder why you never believed you could really enjoy your physicality.

Remember all of the taught behavioral mannerisms that you've experienced, all the thought forms, and honor the dear brothers for their teachings. But something happens once you've decided to go beyond those teachings. You may be a little bit afraid at first because you won't be like anyone else anymore. Maybe you won't fit in. So maybe you will stop trying to fit in and let yourself open up. Letting yourself open, not from a little you, but from the eyes you were just looking through—those of your eternal Beingness, your eternal life. This is You in your eternal bliss coming back to You, through You, as You. Now you're playing with true acceptance and true embodiment and the divinity of Christ consciousness, forever expanding into You.

The acceptance to let yourself be, to experience, and to play with everything is the true acceptance, the love of All That Is and beyond. Everything beyond just the tangible materialistic belongings, they'll come and they'll go, and the same question remains: "Who am I?" you ask. "I'm definitely not the job position or the abundance in the bank. I'm definitely not the washer, or dryer, or the TV, or any other 'thing'. I'm certainly not any of these costumes that I've been taught to identify myself with." You've been taught that you'll wear one thing if you're important, and something else entirely if you're not. Look at all of the power that has been given to these things. What has it really been about anyway? And no matter what you've done or what you do, you've been taught to focus on what's wrong. You've made so many mistakes. But wait a minute! Maybe you haven't been making mistakes. Maybe you've been going through these situations to begin to get your own attention, to understand the emotions such as guilt, frustration, anger, anxiety, and all the other stuff that you are now going beyond.

Ask yourself, "Am I ready to be done with the struggles, inwardly and outwardly? Am I ready to be done with attempting to make things different than the perfection that they are? Am I ready to be done with creating all of these perceptional beliefs in my own consciousness? Am I ready to be done with all the bookwork and all the footwork? Am I ready to be done with carrying all of these big giant loads? Am I ready to be done with all of the struggles to understand myself?" Now what answers do you hear?

When you're coming from a clear state of consciousness, a clear state of heart, a clear state of neutrality, all is available for you. Neutrality is being completely open to everything and being disengaged from what is happening around you, because this is where the availability and enjoyment of everything comes from. A neutral state isn't just an is-ness, isn't just neutrality. It's true wide openness. As you're playing with a clear state with no intent, you can begin to experience yourself and welcome in all opportunities and All That Is presenting for you. Now have a blast! There is nothing to stop you. You're not going to deny your exuberance, your excitement, and what you are doing is letting your life become so much more exciting. This is the true excitement that comes from a state of expansion, of expression, of divinity, of being able to enjoy everything to its fullest.

You're not giving your power away to an outside deity, to the angelic presences, the archangelic realms, or the ascended hosts. As you are embodying yourself now and playing with your guidance realms, you are truly dancing with them, allowing them to give to you and complement you. Allow yourself to enjoy everything, to keep accessing your own innate abilities and exploring them, expressing and expanding beyond the universal law principle, and from your natural state. Allowing is really just letting everything be. And as you're letting things be, you're still just simply showing up for the clarities and opportunities that present. You're simply playing, singing, dancing, and enjoying all of creation. Do you see? Because now that you don't have another job to do, you don't have to <u>try</u> to be allowing, you don't have to <u>try</u> to let everything be. Now can you see that as the divinity that you've always been, you can just let everything take on its own life of its own accord? You're welcoming and giving permission to let life present, showing up in these different scenarios just because they are right there before you.

You don't need to contemplate what you enjoy or don't enjoy, or what you think is fun or not fun. The world has become a whole new playground. Here you are, breaking the metaphoric hijacking and actually taking yourself off of the tightropes created by the old rules, old paradigms. Living beyond the mind, beliefs, identifications, and emotions, you're at a brilliant bridging point able to explore so much more, beyond a comfortability level. You're not pushing but letting everything in your outside world move around before you. What if you didn't even need to be in charge of making choices? Because that's when you're just beginning to wake up from the cause and effect, action and reaction and so forth. And as you're doing that you're going to start to be able to "trust" that everything is going to be okay. You're going to watch what happens.

If you choose to let things be, watch how many miraculous events take place. This is beyond what your mind could have calculated from the limits of its understanding. Based on its past experiences, the mind doesn't have enough information to understand.

Now you know that if you make this decision you'll have this outcome, and if you make that decision you'll have that outcome. But what if you're not making decisions at all? What if you've outgrown choice? What if you've outgrown making the brilliant strategic moves, and on, and on? Of course it's going to take away from some of the emotional excitement, because now you're not going to be putting all of this fragmented energy into decision making. But when you're no longer putting perceptional beliefs into decision making, watch how you feel more vibrant than ever.

And I want to be clear—watch how you feel more uncomfortable. And I mean <u>big time</u> uncomfortable. But why? The reason is that you're going to hear your true calling, this eternal familiarity, your natural state. And although this is your natural state, it is also the unknown, and quite a way beyond your old comfortabilities. By going beyond your comfortability you're playing with expansion and openness. You're letting that place of uncomfortability once again become comfortable. And now, if you're not making a decision you're maintaining neutrality, and you are going with what is being presented from a neutral state. And then you will to start to see the true outcome of events from the eyes of Creator Incarnate.

Let's use the example of a scientist attempting to find the cure for a disease. Based on his own perception of what he has learned, what he's studied and experienced, he believes there will be certain outcomes to his experiments. But what if he said, "Show me what truly is. Show me what the true outcome is without my mind level affecting the outcome." The mind level would put together the list of items, getting together all the microscopes, petri dishes, tubing, and otherwise. Because that is where the mind level excels; that's how it serves you. Now the scientist is going to be able to see beyond veils and beliefs, to see the molecules in the cells. He's going to be wide open, seeing beyond the basic data. Having certain basic data is something of a necessity when playing with science. So he will use what he's already been taught, but he's also going to be open to something completely new. In this way, you're going to let yourself go beyond physics, quantum physics, metaphysics, and go into your neutral state of "Show me the truth."

Seeing the truth is being in the world of reality. Call it true reality. Call it a state that is beyond all perceptions. "Show me the is-ness of what's taking place. Show me the is-ness of an outcome. Show me the missing link that I keep missing precisely because I keep looking for the missing link. Show me what truly is. Show me the beauty of what truly is." So now you can take this brilliant, priceless data and information so much further. And you're able to do so because you stepped out of books. You've stepped out of everything you've been taught, stepped out of all realities. The old realities were so dense; you've let them begin to change over and open up. And as you have let them begin to change over and open up, you free up all the magnetic levels that had been locked in to create an outcome.

Let's remember when you're playing with a belief system, when you were putting in emotion, you've already locked yourself into a whole unfoldment and created a deity that is still not a reality. As you become more identified with your mind, your mind believes its importance, and you begin to believe that you <u>are</u> your mind. Throughout all of your wonderful endeavors of beliefs, emotions and perceptions throughout your life stream, the mind has created all sorts of outcomes that fed the egoic structure to perceive itself to be real. As you no longer feed these perceptions, you become free to see and know the truth of All That Is and how many abilities that you do have available beyond the mind.

Is the mind important? Absolutely, it's important for things like picking out a costume in the morning. The mind is there for your own resonance of enjoyment, when you're playing with all of your options, different color schemes, deciding how well purple goes with pink. The mind is good for all of the physical attributes that you can play with in this world. Honor its abilities, and appreciate what an interesting endeavor it is to fit into a body on a planet. You don't want to deny the mind, but you do want to go beyond it. Your true journey from You, and as You, when all of your gifts and abilities are beginning to resurface, is about following your heart and creativity. This is letting everything be expanded, letting everything be unlocked and opening into a different scene.

As you move beyond the old ways, the old thought patterns, you continually let things open, and open.

All of a sudden you're starting to feel differently about being in a body on a planet. Do you remember the times when everything has seemed so black and white in your mind? Moving beyond the old thought patterns is like introducing color to your world. Haven't many of your past realities been so limited? When I say limited, I mean that they have been less about a journey and more about stagnation. A limit is to settle for what seems to be available rather than exploring what is truly available. And I mean available beyond what brother humanity says or believes is available. What will happen if you let yourself be neutral, expanded, and in a place of is-ness to everything that presents throughout the day? What will happen when you're not locked into a rigid schedule? What will happen when you're letting the trees be the trees, as the beautiful gift they are, the kitties be the kitties, as the beautiful dear brothers they are, and the world be the world, as the beautiful Eden that it is?

This is called freedom from limitations and beliefs. Remember that in the past there were all those egoic emotional perceptions and identities. The ego said, "In order for me to feel good about myself, I need to have certain accomplishments and successes. Oh, and I can't feel good about myself unless I feel bad about someone else." But what if that's no longer the pull? What if you are no longer concerned with the self importance? What if you just show up? Let's have fun with the whole world and call in your higher levels to show you. Show you what gifts today has to offer. How best can you emanate the presence of who you are in the world today, or how best can you let that happen on its own? How best can you give yourself the go-ahead to look at the day for what it truly is while you're walking through it? Now you're starting to play. You're letting life be life. You're letting the world be the world. You're letting the brilliant kingdoms be what they are. You're letting the checkbook be the checkbook, and the accounts be the accounts. You're letting the family be the family.

When the mind has been engaged, the amount in the checkbook means this is what you are worth, and the family means only what you should feel proud or guilty about. You place so much importance on everything. When life is so deadly serious, there is no enjoyment. Now why not ask yourself what would really happen if you are no longer being run by the world and the mind from outside perceptions, jobs, finances, and relationships? Would things be okay? Would it all be taken away? Or could you begin to see, feel, experience, express so much more? Would you be free from the limiting beliefs on the planet?

Yes, you're actually letting things start to move. Now you are waking up from your tunnel vision. You're not just having glimpses of the Universe, but actually expressing, embodying, and experiencing All That Is. Beyond neutrality, beyond is-ness, beyond all of these phrases; you have now come to You. You're truly, completely, fully experiencing, and expressing all of You, and all of creation. As you start to break it down into the experiential realms, some experiences are feeling more exuberant than others. But what if you go even beyond experience and into expression? Because remember, there's been so much that has been believed and embodied. What if you start to play more with the expression of You, beyond another job to do? I'm not suggesting that you're <u>attempting</u> to change anything. What if the changes started taking place automatically just because you gave yourself permission? Not acting, not pretending because this isn't another thing to do, or way to behave. This is You that you're letting come in and through you again.

In this type of world, what would be the difference between running the multi-million dollar business or cleaning out a toilet? There would be no difference whatsoever. Because what is there not to be enjoyed? Without judgment there can be true enjoyment. Now there's not an egoic part that's always saying, "Me, me, me!" You become completely selfless, going beyond the mind and the egoic states of importance. Now, you're going into a whole different paradigm. Consider the Mother Theresa and Mahatma Gandhi scenarios, the perceptional beliefs of the Yeshua bin Joseph (Jesus) scenarios. Whether you are washing feet or whatever you're doing, there is no identity or judgment about it, it is simply going with what is presenting as the love and brilliance of who you are. When you began to wake up and follow your nudges, You made the brilliant decision and opened yourself. And now you come to terms with the fact that, of course you can have everything, be open to everything and beyond without the necessity of walking on the sacrificial altar. There is no such thing as sacrifice.

If you give yourself permission to be You and the presence that you are, you will be going into a whole new world. And then of course the question arises from the mind, "<u>Now</u> where do I fit in?" So I ask you, what would happen if you gave yourself the go-ahead to embody the is-ness and love that you are and you became the difference in the world? Not because you're trying, not as a job to do, or another mission statement or contract. What if you let all of that be complete and resolved? You see, you have made the decision to let yourself be the expression rather than simply the experiencer. Yes, you're having experiences, but you have ceased being either victim or victimizer. You are expressing through this world, and what presents in your life stream is there for your enjoyment and education.

Your clarity can now begin presenting more than ever because you're starting to see things for what they are. And this is so different from that tunnel vision approach of taught behavioral mannerisms, or from the self-conscious deity you've been playing with. Let's say that you want more than anything to communicate with your child. But she remains a mystery to you. And always, always there are the fights and the struggles. Your mind says that this behavior is going to equal that outcome. So you know she will say something to you in front of her friends, and it will hurt your feelings, so you'll get angry and punish her. Because you've heard so many times that the parent has to be in charge. And the old religion has said, "Spare the rod and spoil the child!" But do you see how you're creating the outcome due to past perceptions? At one time things did happen that way, but why does it have to be true today? Start to let yourself be neutral. You see that your behavior <u>and</u> her behavior have been taught and implemented. But neither of you was coming from clarity. What if you become the peace that dissolves the battle?

Call this being clear, if you like. It doesn't really matter what you call it. I call it being You, the real You. You as Creator have been commanding all of these perceptional deities to be real and commanding them to be a concrete reality. Now that you are aware of what you command into reality, you can start to let go. If you contemplate those boxes dear ones put themselves in, you may notice that all of the different beautiful scenarios that you've been looking at have been fed to humanity for eons, handed down through the centuries. You will notice that they all had to do with only two parts—the mind and the body. But these are really not that important anymore because you've woken up from them.

The Universe is neutral. To the Universe the scenarios don't matter, and they never have. And your higher levels have just wanted to love, honor, and support you. They have waited for you to wake up and step into You, for you to remember who You are. So now you have the full complete embracement, your state of embodiment, integrated with your higher and lower self, emanating from your heart center. "As above, so below," the marriage of the higher and lower You can now take place. Of course, there's the little barrier in-between that we've called perceptional emotion, egoic states of consciousness, the mind level. The mind has been given so much power, but you now have the ability to surpass this barrier. What you are truly doing is letting yourself be free.

Now you are living and experiencing a singular egoic structure, as an expression of Beingness that is and has always been You, bypassing the inundation of data, beliefs, identities, and emotional states of consciousness from other egoic structures. So, my offering, my challenge for you is to please, please question everything I'm saying. Question what I'm sharing. Because this is about You remembering You. It's about You embracing You. Because to challenge what I say here assists you to discover who you've always been.

You don't need to re-comfort yourself and re-process all that has happened for good or ill in your life stream. You no longer have to forgive or not forgive. You woke up to your higher levels, a brilliant brotherhood that says, "We want to give you everything. Now let us show you what today looks like. Let us show you what this life stream truly looks like. How best can we assist?" Assisting is a hand up. Assisting is clarity about what you're presented with. And you can assist these other dear brothers around you, the ones you see panicking and struggling. Let's not be afraid of yourself or the situation. You're sharing exactly what's necessary for them; you are what they're asking for. But also, let's not get caught in a societal rule of what can be said or not said, or what can take place or cannot take place. Let's just be in your brilliance and going with what is divinely being presented right in front of you.

There's noone else to blame, noone else to carry. It comes back to You remembering You. But it's not you from "I think, I should, I ought, I must, I have to, I need to, I've got to." It's You as the beauty that you are, the divine brilliance you are, as Creator Incarnate.

Step back for a moment and feel the presence of Creator that you are. For example, let's play with your heart level, the center of your body principle. This is the core of all the chakra level vortexes. As you play with your heart level, open that area of your physicality, open up the right and left atrium and the ventricles of your heart. This is beyond being fluffy. You're not trying to be the love, or the essence, or the divinity. You're not trying to force the good enough/not good enough scenarios. You're not trying to feel blissful, happy, sad; you're not trying to feel your essence.

And now you're going to be feeling such a brilliant sensation throughout your whole physicality because you've waved the white flag. You're surrendering to who You are. You're surrendering—to let yourself succeed, to let yourself have a blast. You're surrendering to letting yourself be cared about and loved within and throughout every level of your being. So in truth, you have also surrendered to yourself, to your higher levels. You have surrendered to the nudge. How empowering does that sound?

The reason it sounds empowering dear one is because it is yourself embodying your <u>true</u> self. You don't have to achieve, or force, or control your egoic structures any longer. Now you're stepping into your true power, the true power that has always been about You, and no longer the false power of dominating or being dominated. What would be the use of that? You would be going right back to recreating a karmic grid system that you have already outgrown. True empowerment is not to have to force anymore. The opening of true power means that you can begin to experience the flowers in the yard for the first time, their expression of brilliance, beauty, nature and freedom. Can you begin to see what is starting to happen? You're no longer being the one holding onto the string of the kite that's been pulling you all over the place. That's what the egoic mind is like, a kite blowing about with every breeze.

So you've let the kite string go. Rather than hold on to it or try to control it, you've let the wind carry the kite away. And now you've let your wings sprout and open, as you move beyond the old realities. Now you are going beyond neutrality and is-ness. You're going beyond your manifest levels, your Creator levels. You're beginning to embody and express the facet of Creator that you are. So let's say you ask yourself, "How best can I begin to express who I am?" And your answer is, "I am one beyond the singular one, and the expression of particles of light consciousness expanding throughout all of creation, beyond the mass magnetic particles that make up forms. I am now one with All That Is, having gone beyond magnetics and beyond the little me. I am openness throughout everything, so I can begin anew to play throughout creation, being in the world but unaffected by it. I am open to the true beauty and magnificence of the world and the total, complete enjoyment of it in all ways, and in all realms."

Wow! That's quite an answer! But let's examine it a bit. You can no longer be confined to certain behavioral mannerisms. And I can promise you this, you're going to have a blast 24/7. You're no longer going to confine yourself or your body vehicle to what you must have or not have, what you must be or not be.

Going beyond taught perceptional judgment and into optimum health, flourishing, and vibrant. You wonder what is next. So what would happen if you didn't have to be in charge of your health either? Wow, this is becoming a little bit scary, isn't it? Absolutely! It is scary because what you've done is step into the abyss of neutrality, the unknown. Do you see that by doing so you've also let everything be okay permanently? You've allowed everything to become extraordinary. Perhaps the biggest gift to yourself is letting your curiosity and enjoyment come back to life. In other words, you've taken the most extraordinary journey to let yourself become You once again. Great job!

This is the beginning of a whole new world, a whole new life, the beginning of complete openness. That's why the Universe and your angelic, archangelic and ascended hosts are celebrating you for letting this re-awakening and remembering take place. They are assisting you to be integrated, amplified, embodied, and embraced. But more than that, this whole Universe, angelic presences, archangelic realms, ascended hosts are asking you to keep going, to let yourself come to life fully. What priceless courage this has taken! Now you no longer have to confine yourself; you can let their presence be acknowledged within your own presence as you dance side by side. Great job! As you get out the champagne and chocolate cake, let's celebrate your accomplishment for giving yourself the permission to fully embody the brilliance that You are.

Let's celebrate the accomplishment of You remembering who you are, the accomplishment of giving yourself the go-ahead and permission to begin to express. But remember that the expression state is not a state of trying or a not trying—it is neutral. How do you express who you are? Ask yourself, "Who am I?" Then watch what presents. You could create a belief about yourself. But when doing that, can you feel the structure and confinement? Even within your body structure? You've been creating beliefs about yourself all your life. Now, when you attempt to explore what has been within you, you will begin to find that there's nothing there to explore that will not be expressed or brought to the forefront. Call it re-examination of yourself. As you begin to celebrate remembering who You are, celebrate getting your own attention, remembering your own essence, your own divinity. Celebrate the brilliant presence that You emanate.

This is where the writing and rewriting of your genetics, your DNA, your cellular vibratory structures, all of it's going to take care of itself. Of course your body structure is going to go through all kinds of changes, and of course you're going to be feeling all sorts of emanating, odd sensations. Your body is beginning to catch up with the embodiment of You on all levels of creation. And remember, it's time to celebrate humanity as a brotherhood. The truth is that humanity has never, ever gotten to this point before. As the karmic grid system continues to break down, you can embrace the changes fully and completely. Now you can give yourself a hug and stand in your own divinity and begin to experience all kinds of fun—things such as true love, abundance, new jobs and new camaraderies. At the same time, what if you also let yourself express the beauty, the excitement, the exuberance of who You are? This is who You are in all your grand magnificence, completely open to all of creation and all the gifts that your higher levels, Creator levels and the Universe have to offer.

And finally, remember this: Neutrality is just scratching the surface.

MEDITATION ON LIVING IN A CLEAR STATE

You may wish to have someone read this meditation to you or record yourself reading it so you can follow along easily. Also, you can do these meditations with or without closing your eyes and over time you may experience that there is no need to close your eyes at all.

Let's bring your consciousness
right through the palms of your hands
all the way up your lower arms
your upper arms
your shoulders
through your neck
all the way down through your sternum
through your heart
through your solar plexus
through your creator chakra level vortex
all the way through your root chakra level vortex
through your upper legs
through your lower legs
out the bottom of your feet
up to your upper arms
lower arms
down your hands

right back through your heart again
bring your consciousness from your heart
through your throat level
through your pineal and pituitary gland levels
through your crown chakra level vortex
bring your consciousness through the atmospheric
realms
all the way to the sun
connecting with the sun
your higher levels
bringing a brilliant stream of light
a brilliant stream of gold
from your higher levels
through the physical level
all the way through your crown chakra level vortex
your pineal and pituitary glands
your throat
all the way down through your heart
and expanding exponentially
throughout the room
throughout the home
throughout the surrounding areas
all the way throughout the cities
the states
the provinces
exponentially throughout the whole planet itself
and let's welcome in your big guns
your higher levels
of creator essence
of creator source
the light beingness
the fusion

let's welcome it forward
speak to me
steer me
journey me
let it continue to grow
and become amplified
and amplified
and amplified
can you feel now where you're separate from the
world
but yet you have not denied the world
you're separate from the chaos
the traumas
the dramas
the beliefs
the perceptions
the emotions
and you're stepping fully and completely into you
through the world
which is being a full complete clear state of
consciousness
and being able to play with the world in this state
to bring yourself home
letting yourself be at home
anywhere and everywhere you're at on the planet
and letting the outside world begin to come to life
to further complement you
as you let yourself be in this clear state
you are also letting everything around you take on its
own life
to further complement you

We invite you to visit www.WilliamLinville.com to receive free video and audio downloads and learn more about our upcoming webcasts, teleconferences, live events, and Mastery Program.

CPSIA information can be obtained at www.ICGtesting.com
Printed in the USA
LVOW05s0815171213

365691LV00046B/651/P